THE LOVES OF MY LIFE

ROSE MELLO

Translated to English:
Beatriz Stella Rueda
Campinas, Brazil, April, 2025

Original Title in Portuguese

"Os amores de uma vida"

© Rose Mello, 2016

World Spiritist Institute

Houston, Texas, USA

E – mail: contact@worldspiritistinstitute.org

About the Medium

Rose Mello was born in São Paulo, SP, and raised in Rio de Janeiro, RJ.

She is a writer and environmental designer with a postgraduate degree in lighting design.

She believes in the beauty of life and in the human capacity to make the world a better place, and believes that faith and connection with positive energies drive and encourage us along the way.

She indicates that she appreciates the arts in general, but maintains a preference for painting, sculpture, and literature.

A voracious reader, she has always sought to learn and read all genres, but today she seeks books that provide a constructive message and enriching content.

She mentions that studying, seeking general knowledge, pursuing personal and professional development, maintaining good ethical conduct, and maintaining values structured through a good education are neither obsolete concepts nor passing fads.

Technology has advanced greatly, some social structures have changed, and we are in the 21st century, but culture, education, and ethics are timeless and should be present in everyone's daily lives. Furthermore, he likes to seek happiness and, above all, always maintain optimism and joy for life.

Synopsis

Rosana is a successful executive holding an important position at the São Paulo branch of a multinational IT company. Beautiful, young, and wealthy, she has always been very practical and rational, managing everything around her with planning and organization.

In her professional life, she had achieved success, which also extended to her personal life. An only child of a farming couple, she had strong bonds of love and respect with her parents. She was loved by her friends and maintained a stable relationship with Roberto, her boyfriend, a doctor who was completely in love with her.

Her life was surrounded by harmony and tranquility.

Until one day, a great storm hits the city, and ends up putting Rosana face to face with a man who has the power to shake her entire solid structure built over the years.

A surreal encounter that throws Rosana off balance and means her life will never be the same. The circumstances of this moment are incredible and lead Rosana to question her own mental health.

From that day on, she will have to face her deepest values, accept and confront her fears, and recognize her fragility in the face of life. Her skepticism will crumble, leaving her unable to deny the facts.

Faced with the challenges posed by the situation, Rosana will discover that within her there is a personality hitherto unknown, just waiting for the right moment to reveal itself.

She will learn about true love, faith, courage, and resignation.

And her greatest grief will outlive herself.

Contents

Chapter 1..7
Chapter 2..16
Chapter 3..27
Chapter 4..39
Chapter 5..46
Chapter 6..56
Chapter 7..66
Chapter 8..73
Chapter 9..82
Chapter 10..93
Chapter 11..105
Chapter 12..116
Chapter 13..126
Chapter 14..140
Chapter 15..151
Chapter 16..164
Chapter 17..177
Chapter 18..190
Chapter 19..194

Chapter 1

The sky was dark and heavy, and a downpour would soon take over the city. When the alarm went off, Rosana looked through the ajar curtain and felt like going back to sleep. With the onset of winter, it was quite cold outside, but the temperature in the bedroom remained pleasant.

She lazily got up, looked in the mirror, ran her hands through her hair and made a face, then laughed. Soon she was enveloped in the hot water of the shower, feeling that the bath had revived her, preparing her for another long day at work.

As she sipped her coffee and ate a slice of white cheese, she reviewed the day's agenda. Her only appointment would be a meeting with a client at ten o'clock and she thought she could take care of personal details after lunch in peace.

Just before eight o'clock, she was ready to leave.

Still in the elevator, she picked up her cell phone and called Roberto:

- Good morning, love, I am leaving. Did you sleep well?

- Hi darling, I did, but as always, I missed you a lot! With a smile she replied:

- I miss you too, but you said yesterday that you would better go home; today you have that lecture at the university, don't you?

- That is true, and I like to be well rested on these occasions. It is amazing how the students always surprise me with sometimes baffling questions - he concluded, laughing.

- Lunch together?

- I will pick you up at the office at 1pm, okay?

- That is fine. See you there and a big kiss.

- Love and think of me. When she got into the car, Rosana turned on the stereo first. The music accompanied her whenever possible and made her feel relaxed and calm, even in the heavy traffic in São Paulo.

The rain was already falling heavily, and the cars were moving slowly along the streets and avenues. Rosana resigned herself to the traffic jam - there was still plenty of time for the meeting - and absent-mindedly began to think about her life. She had graduated early as a Systems Analyst and had soon landed an internship at a large multinational company.

She was thirty years old, and, unlike her college friends, she had not put marriage on her list of priorities. She was a responsible and very competent intern; when she managed to get a permanent position in the company, she opted to rent a small apartment and moved out on her own, with the full support of her parents.

Sometime later, she met Roberto, a pediatrician three years older than her, at a party. He was a sophisticated and handsome man. Tall, dark-haired and with a mustache, a detail that Rosana appreciated very much. They started dating. Their relationship had always been strong and there was a lot of complicity between them, but they decided that they would each continue to live in their own home, which did not stop them from frequently spending the night together at each other's house.

"My life is perfect!" - thought Rosana, feeling a great sense of peace!

Suddenly her thoughts were interrupted by the sound of hail hitting the roof of the car. She looked around and saw that the city was already turning into chaos. Water was rapidly flooding the streets. Rosana pulled the car over at a gas station and decided to call Fernanda, her secretary.

- Nanda, Rosana. How are you?

- All calm, Rosana. Where are you? The rain is awful, and the water has risen a lot here in the street.

- I'm still a little far away - replied Rosana, trying to analyze the situation. Has anyone called?

- Not yet. What do you want me to do? Do you think it is better to cancel the meeting?

- It might be more convenient. Leave a new date open, okay?

- Don't worry, I will sort everything out here. Just take care, because the city gets crazy in this weather.

- OK! I will be there soon. See you soon.

When she hung up the phone, Rosana realized that the situation was even worse. The sky was very dark, and the lights in the streets, offices and stores began to come on. There was no way she could continue her way. She parked in a space at the gas station, grabbed her handbag and got out of the car. It was windy and she ran to the convenience store that was sheltering several people who had also left their cars. Since she had to wait, she would have something to drink. She poured herself a coffee, picked up a magazine and started reading. Every now and then she looked outside, but nothing had changed; perhaps it was going to take longer than expected. She thought about calling Roberto, but gave up when she remembered that he should have started his talk by now.

She had been there for more than twenty minutes. She closed the magazine and saw that everyone was relatively quiet, indicating that there was really nothing left to do but wait. It was at that moment that a man walked through the store door. She naturally turned to look and when she saw him, she felt her legs go weak and her chest tighten so much that it felt like she had been punched very hard. Her breathing became difficult, and she gasped for breath, and a dizziness made her support herself so as not to fall.

- "What in God's name?" - thought Rosana, completely disoriented.

Suddenly it was as if it was just the two of them in the room; she could not hear a single sound and saw no one around her. He walked towards the cashier and, as he approached Rosana, asked to be excused.

She said nothing, nor could she move. He looked at her and spoke again in a deep but extremely soft voice:

- Hi, can you excuse me please? It is crowded here, isn't it? She remained still for a few seconds and then slowly moved away.

- Sorry - was all she managed to say with great difficulty.

- Imagine - he replied with the most charming and wonderful smile Rosana had ever seen. He went to the counter, bought something and headed for the exit, without another glance at her. Rosana, without thinking, followed him. She saw him run towards the building next to the gas station and disappear through the large glass doors at the entrance. Rosana walked almost staggering back to the store and, still outside, leaned against the wall. Unable to understand and unable to bear the feeling any longer, she fell into convulsive, uncontrollable weeping. A few people noticed how she was, but no one approached her. She cried a lot, until her eyes began to swell shut and a severe pain took hold of her entire head. Only then did she begin to regain her self-control; She reached into her bag for a handkerchief, dried her face to pull herself together and lifted her head, inhaling so deeply that she seemed to want all the air in the world for herself. She still felt dizzy, and her body was so relaxed now that it seemed anesthetized. She went into the store and bought a bottle of water. Just then another girl approached her and asked:

- Excuse me, but... are you all right? Do you need anything?

- No, thank you. It is just a bad feeling that has passed. I need to go. Thanks again. The girl did not insist, and Rosana went back to her car. She did not turn on the stereo! She sat with her head resting on the seat.

- I cannot understand - she asked herself in anguish. Who was that man? What was my reaction? Am I going mad?

She could not organize her thoughts, but she was certain of one thing: she could not go to work under these conditions.

She called Fernanda again, trying hard to disguise her state of mind.

-Nanda, it is me again. It looks like the storm is passing, but I think it is still going to be difficult to get to the office...

Did you manage to talk to the people at the meeting? Was there a problem canceling it? - she spoke slowly.

- No, Rosana, they were even about to call and cancel everything. The new date was left open as you asked, and they thought it was great. Is everything all right with you?

- Everything is fine, Fernanda; I just got a migraine, and I am going to take the

opportunity to rest at home.

- I will let anyone know that you are not coming today. Take care of yourself because I know all about these migraine attacks.

Fernanda hung up, but she felt something was wrong. Rosana only called her by name when she was very worried about something. She used to affectionately call her Nanda. They had worked together for a long time, which strengthened a mutual sympathy that turned into a good friendship. She was apprehensive, but as she always did, she tried to forget about it and talked to Rosana at the first opportunity.

There was great respect between them, and they used to talk about the most varied subjects. They shared confidences, sorrows and happiness. But in the workplace, they tried to maintain a very professional relationship, avoiding intrigue and gossip. Over time, they got to know each other so well that it was not unusual for them to communicate with just a glance.

Fernanda would wait for Rosana to come to her to get things off her chest. But in any case, she would call her in the evening just to see if her friend was all right.

Rosana drove as if she were on autopilot. At times she thought she would not be able to get out of the car. When she entered the building garage, she felt like a survivor. She turned off the car and once again she was too exhausted to move. Her body heavy and her head aching, she got out and took the elevator. When she entered the apartment, she threw her keys and handbag on the table, went into the bedroom and collapsed on the bed. She remained stagnant, her gaze fixed on the ceiling... She could not understand it, but she was suffering a lot, a pain she had not known before. Tears started rolling down her cheeks again, but she did not bother to hold them back. She wanted to cry, to get that immense sadness out. She turned on her side, hugged her pillow and fell asleep.

She woke up to the phone ringing, but did not feel like getting up to answer it. The answering machine activated and recorded a message that she would hear later.

Her heart was tight, but sleep had improved her general condition considerably. She got up and went to take a shower. She lay still for a few minutes, letting the water run over her body as if to take the weight off her. She got out and put on a robe, dried her long brown hair lightly and went into the living room.

The curtains were closed, and she preferred to leave them that way, lighting only the small lamp on the table next to the sofa. She walked over to the bookcase and put on a CD; the soft, slow music filled the apartment. He lay down on the sofa and only then began to think about everything in a more analytical way.

What had happened was not normal, that much was clear. Had it been what they call love at first sight? "No" - she thought with conviction! Everything she knew about love was nothing like what she had felt.

When you see someone, you are immediately attracted to, you can feel your heart racing, your hands shaking, your eyes glazing over... but what she felt was an impact, a shock..."THAT!" - she concluded victoriously. It was a very strong shock indeed. But... why? She had never seen that man before in her life. The memory of his image was clear in her mind, as if he were standing right there in front of her. And what a smile! He was a spectacle, perhaps the most handsome man she had ever seen!

What nonsense - she analyzed, getting up to go to the kitchen. Much better- looking men were on every movie screen all over the world... but... she did not know what... he was very special. Would she have been impressed by his beauty? Not either! That would have left her awestruck at most.

She grabbed a coffee, opened a drawer and took out a pack of cigarettes and a lighter. She should have given up this terrible addiction once and for all, but she was still a long way off.

As she returned to the sofa, she remembered the phone call she had received and went to listen to it.

- "Oh my God!" - she sighed in anguish. It was Roberto, very worried because she had not heard from him, had not shown up for lunch and had disappeared. She picked up the phone and called his cell, hoping that the call would be transferred to voicemail. Bingo! She heard the message to leave a message:

-Roberto, forgive me love! I got stuck in the middle of the storm, had to cancel the morning meeting and ended up having one of my migraine attacks. I have decided to go home. I will rest in the afternoon, and I will call you in the early evening. Big kiss. She felt relieved that she did not have to talk to him now. What was she going to say? That she was going crazy and having a tantrum in the street because of a stranger?

She lit her cigarette and returned to the sofa. She was calm now and watched the smoke without thinking about anything. But soon the image of that smile came back to her mind... that word spoken in a wonderful voice - "Imagine" - he had said simply, but to her it sounded like a beautiful song. And then her eyes filled with tears and the tightness in her heart returned.

She put out her cigarette, closed her eyes and squeezed them tightly shut; she wanted to push the memory away.

-"What's happening to me?" - she thought again, becoming restless. She searched her memory and tried to recall some occasion; some place where she might have seen that face. Some unpleasant situation she might have witnessed involving that man... nothing! She had never seen him.

Very tired, she decided to stop fighting and everything came back to her mind... His face, his physique, his voice... everything so perfect... and thinking, for the first time she smiled a little!

She decided it would be better to sleep again until the evening, and that is what she did. And she dreamt!

He was with her, but they did not come close. They looked at each other with tenderness and love; she tried to get close, to touch him, but she could not. When she tried to speak to him, her voice would not come out. When she tried to speak to him, her voice would not come out. He blew her a kiss and gradually disappeared. She tried to follow him, but she could not move.

She stirred for a few moments and then fell back into a deep sleep. There was no dream... everything was dark!

Chapter 2

It was late at night when Rosana woke up. She was surprised by the lateness of the hour. For the first time that day, she felt a huge emptiness in her stomach and realized how hungry she was. It was just as well: her last meal had been in the morning.

Her answering machine was flashing with messages. She began to listen to them. A dry cleaner telling her that her dress was ready; a call with no message; her mother just wanting to say hello; a friend inviting her to a party at the weekend; a call with no message; Fernanda.

She needed to eat something first; then she would return the calls. She went to the kitchen and prepared a sandwich of smoked turkey breast, white cheese, tomato and lettuce. She seasoned it with some herbs. She opened the fridge and took out the jug of lemonade. No, that was not what he wanted to drink. She put the jug away again and grabbed a bottle of pear juice.

She went into the living room and turned on the TV. The evening news was on. She watched without interest, but the news distracted her thoughts. When she had finished eating, she brushed her teeth, lit a cigarette and picked up the phone.

- Hi Mom, are you having dinner?

- No, my child, we are finished. Today is our bridge day with Liana and Eduardo, have you forgotten?

- Oh, that is right. Have they arrived yet? Tell them I am sending them a hug. Is Dad well?

- Yes, he is as cheerful as ever. When are you coming over?

- Maybe tomorrow night. I had a bad day today because of the rain.

- What? I didn't even leave the house. Darling, they are already calling me. I will talk to you tomorrow.

- Enjoy your evening, Mom, and a kiss to everyone. Now I'll call Fernanda.

- No, I would better call Roberto straight away. I had been very rude and - he did not deserve it.

- Rosana, I am so glad you called. I was about to leave to go to your house. How are you?

- My love, I am sorry about today. It has been a very complicated day. I have only just woken up. I am feeling much better and the migraine is gone.

- Do you want me to come and stay with you? Do you need anything?

- No, my dear, /don't worry. I am going to read a bit and try to sleep again. Tomorrow, I want to be in a good mood to get my work done.

- Have you seen the weather forecast in the paper? It looks like it is going to be much nicer tomorrow, so how about we meet up for the lunch we missed today?

- Perfect, and I am sure it will all work out - she concluded with a smile.

And / don't schedule anything for the evening; I will need a lot of time by your side to heal all the homesickness I am feeling.

-I miss you too. Tomorrow, I will not let you go, you can be sure of that. They hung up affectionately and Rosana was anxious to talk to Fernanda.

After a quick chat, they decided that Fernanda would go to her friend's house. Rosana went up to her room and while she was choosing comfortable clothes, she was thinking about how she was going to tell Fernanda what had happened. It was all too surreal, and she felt a bit ridiculous. She put on a navy blue and white sweatshirt, brushed her hair and put it up in a ponytail. She looked at herself in the mirror: given everything she had been through; she looked pretty good. The doorbell rang.

- Fernanda - said Rosana, welcoming her friend in a big hug.

- Rosana, you have got me worried. I thought something more than a migraine was tormenting you, but I did not want to be too hasty and say anything over the phone.

- You know me very well, my friend. But you can be sure that what I must tell you goes far beyond your imagination.

- I am already starting to get anxious. What happened that was so horrible?

- Sit here and get ready to listen - said Rosana, pulling her friend by the hand to the sofa. On the way, she picked up two glasses of wine. Gradually and very calmly, Rosana began to recount the episode at the gas station in as much detail as she could remember. At times, she felt a lump begin to form in her throat and she found it difficult to speak again. But she managed to tell everything without letting the emotion overwhelm her again.

At the end of the story, Fernanda was dumbfounded, not sure if she had understood everything.

- Wait, friend, you don't/do not know this person? Are you sure you have never seen him before?

- Absolutely!

- But from what you have said, your reaction seems to be that of a person who meets someone with whom you have had a very unpleasant experience.

- That is what I thought - interjected Rosana, happy to see that her friend was not thinking she was crazy, at least not completely.

- But if you have never seen him before, it does not make sense!

- None, and that distresses me. You know I have always been a sensible person, with my feet firmly on the ground. It has been very difficult to come to terms with what has happened.

- And now, at this moment, what do you feel when you think of him? Rosana hesitated:

- Longing, a longing so great that it hurts... And I feel afraid. Very afraid!

Fernanda was silent and thoughtful. Rosana got up and went to pour them both some more wine.

- Rosana, I don't know what to say. I have never seen anything like it. You say it was not an attraction, and to tell you the truth, I agree with that; but at the same time, I cannot understand it. What do you intend to do now?

- What can I do? All I can do is try to put a lid on it and forget about it. I don't know who he is, where he is from, nothing! - replied Rosana, but without feeling any conviction in what she was saying - besides, I don't really have to do anything. That man does not interest me; I love Roberto, we are happy, I have never thought of getting involved with anyone else.

Fernanda looked at her suspiciously and Rosana continued:

- What happened is inexplicable, so there is no point in looking for reasons. I am not going to see him again, that is for sure. At that moment, Rosana could no longer hold back her tears. Fernanda hugged her silently, but she was very worried about her friend's state.

-The truth is that when he walked in, it was as if I was seeing the most important man in my life again - Rosana said tearfully.

- It hurt so much to stand in front of him... I was sure, within seconds, that I was standing in front of someone I thought I would never meet again in my life. I am completely devastated, I feel like I am going to explode with despair.

-Rosana, do you believe in reincarnation? We never talk much about beliefs and religion. Drying her tears with a handkerchief, Rosana said:

- No Fernanda, I don't believe in those things. I believe that there is a greater force, which I don't know if it comes from God, that moves the world. But reincarnation, spirits, I really don't believe in that.

- Maybe you are wrong, Rosana. I believe that when we die, we go to another dimension; I don't believe that death is the end of everything. What would be the point of life if everything ended like that?

- But the meaning of life is in life itself. In what we build, in the person we are, in our achievements.

- And why do you think there are so many inequalities in the world?

- That is what I said Fernanda, it depends on our achievements, our effort; if you don't fight for what you want, you will not succeed.

- But do you think that a person born into extreme poverty is going to have the same conditions to achieve what you have achieved, for example? Rosana was baffled.

- That is what I am saying, Rosana. There must be a more satisfactory explanation for such seemingly unfair things. And I think that explanation lies precisely in the question of reincarnation, karma, past lives. I cannot say much either, as I have never delved into this subject. Rosana remained thoughtful, trying to analyze what she had heard.

- And I think, Rosana, that the episode you experienced may have an explanation in this sense. I don't see any other way of understanding a reaction like the one you had. Unless you were suffering from some kind of imbalance, and we know that your mental health is in perfect condition.

- Is that so? - replied Rosana, trying to laugh at her own tragedy. They both laughed together, and the mood became lighter again.

They managed to put the subject aside for a while, and Fernanda told Rosana how the day at the office had gone.

Rosana was highly regarded in the company for her competence and ease of getting what she wanted from clients. She was friendly, intelligent and persuasive, as well as having a deep knowledge of the area in which she worked. She had won major accounts, and this meant that her rise had been structured on secure and definitive foundations.

She was considered a great person, good-hearted and sensitive, but always with ideas based on reality and scientific evidence. Esotericism, spirituality, things like that did not attract her attention.

They took the opportunity to organize their schedule for the next day, and it was almost midnight when Fernanda left. They had not touched on the subject of that mysterious meeting again.

The next day dawned cold but without rain. After a good night's sleep, Rosana woke up in good spirits. All that remained was the feeling that it had all been a crazy dream. She preferred to ignore the memories and went confidently about her daily routine.

She arrived at the office and shortly afterwards had a meeting with the client from the day before. The conversation ended with yet another professional success, and when the visitors left, there was a small celebration for, yet another good deal closed. Rosana was happy.

Fernanda, unlike her friend, could not stop thinking about what had happened, and she was sure that Rosana was concealing her feelings. But she swore to herself that if it were up to her, she would not bring it up again.

At lunchtime, Roberto stopped by to pick Rosana up. They went to a nearby restaurant, where everyone already knew them.

- Rosana, how nice to be here! Yesterday I was very worried about you and sad that I did not see you.

- Please Roberto, let's forget about yesterday! Roberto was surprised by his girlfriend's attitude, after all, nothing much had happened to make her talk so seriously. But he did not take it too seriously.

- How is your day today, love? Any more lectures at the university?

- No. I have several appointments in the afternoon, and I am not due to leave the office until early evening. Would you like me to bring something for dinner? How about watching a DVD?

- Perfect! But don't worry, I will make us something to eat; maybe that pasta sugo you like?

- Do you have a preference for the movie, or can I pick it up at the video store?

- Take what you think is good; today I want to watch anything, and I love all genres, you know. I have to call my mom. I said I might drop by her house tonight. Roberto frowned. Rosana laughed, winked, picked up her cell phone and called her mother to tell her she could not make it.

They spent the rest of lunch talking about various topics, laughing a lot and exchanging affection.

When Roberto left her at the office, he said:

- Rosana, I am the happiest man in the world to have you! Do you know how much I love you?

- Roberto, I love you too - she replied, bringing her lips close to his.

He kissed her, feeling his heart beating fast. They had been together for so long, but what he felt was just as intense as it had been at the start of their relationship. They arranged to meet in the evening at her house.

When she arrived in her office, Rosana found Fernanda sitting pensively.

- What is up, Nanda? Is something wrong?

-The usual Rosana - she replied with a slightly sad smile.

- Ah ... Gilberto! - concluded Rosana with an air of disapproval. She sat down next to Fernanda and prepared herself to listen and probably disagree with something. Fernanda was a great person, fun and responsible. She did not have any major problems. But one of her problems was definitely Gilberto. They had been dating for just over a year. He was devoted and passionate. But he felt he owned Fernanda. He was very jealous and if he could, he would certainly spend all day with her. He would pick her up for lunch every day and would often arrange to stop by the office in the afternoon for a snack. A Physical Education teacher, he was not the muscular type. On the contrary, he was slim, with well-defined muscles and slightly graying hair. He wore a beard and moustache and was a handsome man. Perhaps because he was jealous of Fernanda, he was not very friendly with her friends, not even with Rosana. He was not rude, but he was reserved and did not talk much. Fernanda used to be embarrassed by his manner and tried to make him more comfortable in her social environment, and he did not try very hard to help her with this. But she truly loved him and was already learning to deal with her boyfriend's temper.

They talked a lot, and Rosana tried not to give too much of her opinion when it came to their relationship, because Fernanda complained about Gilberto's jealousy, but always ended up acting the way he wanted her to. If she felt happy like that, Rosana would not be the one criticizing what she wanted.

By the time Fernanda left Rosana's office, she was feeling better and more cheerful. They worked quietly for the rest of the day and Rosana finished a little early. She went home to prepare dinner. The traffic was slow, as it always is during rush hour, but that did not bother her. Listening to music, she thought about it again, and once more she felt that tightness in her heart. What was this longing? She could not get rid of that anguish any longer, even though she had been trying hard to forget it all day. She could not stop the memory of him from occupying her mind. On the contrary, she struggled to remember any more details, and as she thought, she smiled and felt invaded by an immense wave of love. Without realizing it, she gave herself over to that feeling. Now she did not want to forget. And she decided: she would go back to the gas station to try to see him again. She had no idea what she would do next, but she would worry about one thing at a time.

When Roberto arrived, dinner was already ready. As he entered, he barely let her close the door. He covered her in kisses and hugs. He poured two glasses of wine and before they had finished drinking, he took her in his arms, carried her to the bedroom and loved her intensely.

While Roberto went to take a shower, Rosana went to the kitchen to heat up the pasta dish. One of her habits was to always shower alone. As soon as Roberto had finished, she asked:

- Roberto, can you take a look at the pasta while I shower? I will not be long.

- No problem! In the meantime, I will pour us some more wine. While in the shower, Rosana thought about how wonderful it always was to make love to Roberto. But tonight, something happened differently. She had enjoyed it, he was affectionate and knew how to put her in the clouds, but it seemed that she had not been whole, had not given herself completely. She sighed and got out of the bath. They talked over dinner, but Rosana tried very hard to pay attention to everything he said. She could no longer control her thoughts and was happy when Roberto decided to put on the DVD. The movie was called "Back to Dying", and it starred Kenneth Branagh and Emma Thompson. It began without holding Rosana's attention. It told the story of a woman who had lost her memory, and of a journalist who found her and was trying to help her unravel the mystery surrounding her life. But at a certain point, Rosana realized that the film was talking about karmic redemptions, past lives, and she stayed tuned until the end. When the movie ended, Roberto began to caress her.

- Honey, let's go to the bedroom? I want you so much - he said softly in her ear. Rosana affectionately kissed him on the cheek and asked him not to be upset, but she was sleepy and all she wanted now was to sleep.

Even though he was disappointed, he respected her wish and they both went to bed. Roberto kissed her and switched off the lamp. In the dark, Rosana kept her eyes open.

Now she was determined to meet that man again. Her reaction that night with her boyfriend had shown that she could not ignore what had happened. She was going to go back to that place; maybe she would be lucky. What intrigued her most was how she felt when she saw him. Maybe if she could get to him, something would become clearer.

Should she tell Fernanda about her intentions? Would she have her friend's support?

Well, she would see the next day.

This time, she projected his image into her room and slept happily!

Chapter 3

Rosana arrived at the office very agitated and motioned for Fernanda to go to her office, then asked her to close the door.

- I am very anxious. I am going back to that place!

Fernanda sat down without showing any surprise.

- I knew you would! Yesterday, I was not convinced by your way of putting a stone on the matter. But what is the point of you going back there?

- I have no idea, but let's analyze it together: I saw him going into that commercial building next to the gas station; he was not carrying any work files, nothing. That could mean that he works in that building and that he came down just to buy something, do you not think?

Fernanda replied, laughing:

- Elementary, my dear Watson!

Rosana grimaced and said:

Please do not laugh, because it is serious! Besides, you will have to think of some excuse to give Gilberto for not having lunch with him today!

-What? - Fernanda said in amazement.

-Why am I not having lunch with him?

- Simple, dear Sherlock: because you are going back to the gas station with me! - she concluded with a wink. Fernanda tried to react but realized that there was no point in arguing; when Rosana got something into her head, it was difficult to dissuade her from the idea. The worst thing would be convincing Gilberto. Near lunchtime, Rosana was impatient. She had already called Roberto and told him that she would have to leave the office for part of the afternoon. As this was common, he did not even ask where she was going. It was more complicated with Fernanda. Gilberto wanted to know at all costs what she was going to do. Fernanda explained that they needed to look at some material for a client, but he could stop by and pick her up for a snack in the afternoon.

Despite everything, Gilberto respected his girlfriend's work very much, and even though he was upset, he had to agree not to meet her for lunch. Rosana went in and out of her office impatiently, and just before noon, she came up to Fernanda, picked up her bag and put it on the table. Her friend laughed, stood up and saluted. Rosana pulled her away, both of them laughing.

They talked a lot all the way. As they got closer, Rosana felt that pain in her chest again but now accompanied by a total heart failure.

As they got out of the car, Rosana ran her eyes all over the place. They went into the store, got two sandwiches and two juices and leaned against the counter in front of the door.

Fernanda thought it was crazy, but she also thought it was funny. There was less traffic that day, and Rosana began to worry.

- I don't think it is going to come to anything, my friend. It would be very lucky if the door opened now, and he came in.

- I am sorry, Rosana, but I don't think that is going to work either. Come to think of it, he might not even work next door. Rosana tapped her hand lightly on the counter and exclaimed:

- Of course, that is it! Instead of staying here, let's go to the building! Fernanda could not believe her ears:

- You are kidding! And what are we going to do there? Ask the doorman where the wonderful man who put you out of your mind is? - she said, her eyes wide.

- Of course not! We are going to look at every floor, room by room - and she stuck her tongue out at her friend, pulling her by the hand again. The entrance had a large counter where visitors had to identify themselves after confirming where they were going. You could not just walk in. The two of them stepped back and stood at the entrance, just watching. There was a certain amount of movement due to the lunch hour... but he did not appear.

- Rosana, you look like a teenager!

- I know, and I am feeling silly. We have been here for over an hour; of course this cannot work - concluded Rosana despondently.

- What am I going to do, Nanda? I must see him again or I will go crazy!

-Calm down; let's go back to the office. We will find a better solution, some good idea. The two of them walked towards the car and Rosana kept looking back. Fernanda felt sorry for her friend.

For the rest of the day, Rosana was unable to work properly. Fernanda, knowing about her condition, tried to do everything she could to avoid disturbing her, including avoiding making unimportant calls.

From the large window in her office, Rosana watched. She loved that city, its grandeur, but now she knew that somewhere in that immensity he existed, and it would be almost impossible to find him again. A tear ran down her cheek. She did not care about anything else. All she wanted was to look at that face again, to touch it, to feel it. She wanted to see him more than anything else in the world.

- "I cannot lose him!" - she thought with great pain in her heart.

- "I cannot be without him again!"

She was not even aware of her own thoughts.

The rest of the day passed slowly, and for the first time in her life, Rosana felt work was too heavy a burden.

At the end of the day, she called Roberto:

- Hi... how was your day?

- Hi, darling. Everything went well, except that I have two more appointments today.

- I am going out soon... and I am having dinner at my parents' house.

- All right; will you come over later? - Roberto asked, finding his girlfriend a little distant.

- No, love, not today. I would rather go straight home. I will see you tomorrow, okay?

Roberto was now convinced that something was wrong, but his next patient was about to come in and he did not want to broach the subject over the phone. He answered coldly:

- That is fine with me, Rosana. I am going to enjoy the evening and stop by the house of a friend I owe a visit to. Call me tomorrow when you can. Rosana did not understand Roberto's manner.

- I will call you then! A kiss and good night.

- Kiss.

When he hung up, Roberto thought for a few moments. There had never been any secrets between them, and their relationship was very open. The next day he would talk to her and everything would be clear.

Rosana passed Fernanda waving and gave her a tired look. She smiled back, sent a kiss and said she would call later.

Rosana's parents' house was cheerful, and they were always very affectionate with her. During dinner, Mr. Otavio watched his daughter carefully. He realized that hidden behind her smile was a great sadness. They sat in front of the fireplace, the father in his usual armchair and Rosana on the floor at his feet, her head resting on his leg. Her mother had gone to the telephone. Stroking her daughter's hair, he asked:

-I know you are not well, my darling. Is there anything I can do to help?

Rosana looked at her father with a twinkle in her eye:

- No, Dad, I don't think so. At least not now - she replied, snuggling closer to him.

- Do not worry. Something is really bothering me, but if I cannot get out of this, I will ask for help. I know I can always count on you and Mom. But you can be sure it is nothing serious - she smiled, trying to reassure her father.

On the way home, Rosana instinctively took a detour and headed in another direction. Before long, she was back where she had only seen him once before. There was no movement. Rosana pulled the car over. She stared into the emptiness, lost in thought.

- "What am I doing?" - she asked herself in anguish.

Feeling angry with herself, she shifted into gear and drove home. As she entered her apartment, the phone was ringing. She ran just in time to answer the call:

- Hi Nanda. I have only just arrived.

- You were with your parents, weren't you? Was everything all right? How are you? She almost did not have the courage to answer:

- I just got back from there...

- Yes, from your parents' house... - Fernanda said hesitantly.

- No... you know where...

Fernanda slumped in her chair:

- Rosana again? At this hour? You must forget all this. I am starting to think that this situation might be doing you too much harm. Were you with Roberto today?

- No... I did not feel like seeing him!

- You see, my friend? All this is messing with your life. You had better stop. My grandmother always said:

- "Whatever has to be, will be".

Rosana was silent for a few moments.

- I do not know if I will be able to forget. Do you not understand? What happened was unique! I know there is something linking me to that man. I need to find out what it is, otherwise, I will not have any peace - she said, feeling agitated.

- I still do not know how, but with every passing minute, I am more certain that I will see him soon.

- Rosana, I am sorry, but I do not know how to help you. Anyway, you know you can count on me unconditionally. Try to rest now. How about lunch together tomorrow?

- What about Gilberto?

- He has gotten another student, and he will have to see him at lunchtime.

- Okay, then. I will talk to you in the morning.

Rosana looked around and found her apartment much bigger than it really was and realized that, despite the affection of her parents, her friends and even Roberto, she was completely alone. She could not share what she was feeling with anyone else. Fernanda tried hard to understand, but Rosana knew it was almost impossible; she herself was completely stunned by recent events.

She was afraid of what she might have to face, but nothing could change her mind. The phone brought her back to reality. It was Fernanda again:

- I cannot stop thinking about everything you are going through. I need to ask you a question - she said cautiously.

- When you met, did you notice any indication in him that he also felt something like what you felt? - she said this afraid to hear the answer.

Rosana replied sadly:

- No... he said those few words very naturally, walked past me and then did not even look at me again. Fernanda had imagined that this would be the answer.

- You may be hurt by what I am about to say, but I think that what happened may not have anything to do with him. I do not know how to explain it, but I think you would better not fantasize about it. You are already suffering too much!

- I was just thinking about this; I appreciate your love and care for me, but I know how difficult it is for you to understand. I cannot go back.

Fernanda did not insist. She said goodbye to her friend with an affectionate word and hung up.

That night Rosana did not cry, she did not miss him, she did not think... that night she allowed herself to feel nothing! She just wanted time to pass quickly... and the day to meet her again to come soon...

Since joining the company, Rosana had never been late. That is why Fernanda looked restlessly at her watch. Her friend should have been in the office for almost two hours. She tried Rosana's cell phone, but it was switched off. At home, she only answered the answering machine. On an impulse, Fernanda picked up the phone book and looked for the name of the gas station where she had been with Rosana. She found it easily. She then called the convenience store:

- Good morning. Please, could you help me? A friend of mine was meeting me this morning and called me to say she was having car trouble. She told me she was near the gas station and would try to solve the problem. But I am trying to reach her on her cell phone, and I cannot get through. Could you check if there is a red station wagon parked there? Sorry to bother you, but it is really important.

- No, madam, I will check, just a minute - said the store assistant attentively. A few minutes later she returned:

- Madam, I could not find it, but a gas attendant said that a car with those characteristics had been here. He even asked the girl driving if she needed anything, but she said no. She just stood there for more than half an hour and drove off. Fernanda thanked him and hung up feeling tense.

Roberto was surprised when he opened the door of his office to say goodbye to a patient and saw Rosana sitting in the waiting room. Surprise soon gave way to happiness and satisfaction. He asked his secretary for two coffees and water, held out his hand to Rosana and led her to his office. When they entered, he pulled her close and kissed her. At that moment, she hugged him tightly and he returned the embrace with love. The secretary knocked lightly on the door and entered, leaving the cups and glasses on the table. As soon as she left, Roberto hugged Rosana again:

- Darling... my love! I could not have imagined starting my day so well. What a delight to see you here first thing in the morning. He was so happy that he could not think about the conversation they had had the day before.

Rosana felt embarrassed; she was not sure why she had gone there. But she did not let her boyfriend notice.

- Sorry about last night!

He sat down with her on the sofa.

- Rosana, I have not felt that you have been very well in recent days - he said frankly.

- I am having a few problems at work, nothing I cannot handle. But until everything is right, I am worried.

- Darling, how long has it been since you have had a few days off? You have not had a vacation in almost two years.

- Maybe it is time to talk it over with João Paulo. Maybe I am going through a process of burnout.

- As a doctor, I can say with certainty that you are on the way to doing just that. I know you love your job, but you need to take care of your health first. Instead of calming down in the face of Roberto's affection, she began to feel guilty... she knew that her problem was not professional! They talked some more and Rosana, claiming she had to go to work, said goodbye with a promise to get together in the evening.

As soon as she left, Roberto took a call:

- Hi Roberto, it is Fernanda. I need to speak with Rosana, but I cannot find her on her cell phone. Did you speak with her today?

- She just left here and said she was going to the office - he replied cheerfully -she should be there soon.

Fernanda said goodbye, sighing with relief. She knew where Rosana was, and Roberto's satisfaction meant that everything was fine between them. But the change in routine, her absence from the company for most of the morning and the lack of news, made her think that all this calm was only apparent. And she was right!

More than two weeks passed, and Rosana tried to keep her life in order, despite the inner turmoil she was experiencing. Fernanda always tried to be attentive and ready to help, but she would not talk about it unless Rosana took the initiative.

Everything was difficult and seemed meaningless. She felt no pleasure in anything, and her meetings with Roberto were turning into moments of distress and guilt.

Every day she found a way to get back to the gas station. She even went there three times in one day. All the employees already knew her. On one occasion, she thought about talking to the store manager, describing the man and asking for some information. But embarrassed by the situation, she gave up.

After almost a month, Rosana began to think that she had been in some kind of delirium, that this man did not exist and that she really needed to rest, or the next step would be medical treatment.

She decided that she would talk to João Paulo, the director of her department, and take a few days' vacation. Maybe she would travel. Leaving São Paulo at that moment could be the solution to getting this episode out of his life for good and he received Fernanda's full support. In two days, she arranged everything so that nothing would go wrong in her absence.

She and Roberto talked a lot, and he thought she would come back refreshed after this time to take care of herself. He would miss her too much, but he recognized that she needed to completely disconnect from her work; if she stayed in São Paulo, she might not be able to. They spent the last night before Rosana's first day off together in his apartment, and she felt very bad that she was relieved when they said goodbye in the morning. He just asked her to let him know as soon as she had decided where she was going.

He called Fernanda early in the morning and even picked her up from home:

- Friend, now it is time to take care of me. You can be sure that you will be surprised when I come back. I will erase all that and be myself again.

-Do you know when and where you are going?

I have not decided, but I will let you know when I do. I am going to hit the road and drive aimlessly. I know it will be great.

- Godspeed and take care. Call me anytime, anywhere if you need to. I will be here cheering you on. Rosana felt tears coming but held back... needed to forget! She packed a large bag with enough clothes for ten or fifteen days, everything very simple and basic. She had no certain destination, but it would be somewhere quiet and private. She put two books in her bag and put her cell phone away. She checked the whole apartment, making sure everything was locked and turned off. When she passed the living room, she picked up a few CDs and left. The afternoon was cold, and the sky overcast, and Rosana found the weather pleasant. She headed off in no particular direction. The city now seemed different to her; she had the impression that half the population had disappeared.

-I would go back just once more - she thought resolutely. It would be goodbye! The end!

She felt an enormous weight on her heart as she got out of the car. She went into the store and stared at the products on the shelves, not really paying attention to anything. She stayed like that for about fifteen minutes; she ended up picking up some cereal bars and left. As she was opening the car door, she saw him. He was walking calmly towards the store.

Rosana's whole-body shook, and her heart felt like it was going to explode in her chest. He entered the store, and Rosana stayed where she was, trying to think of something as quickly as possible. She had to get closer somehow.

Chapter 4

Rosana got into the car, took a brush from her handbag and straightened her hair. She looked at herself in the mirror and thought she looked good. She hurriedly closed the door and went into the store. She did not have time to worry too much about her appearance right now, even though she fervently wanted to be the most beautiful woman in the world.

She was amazed at her sudden self-control, but achieving her goal depended on it.

He was having a snack and did not seem to be in any hurry. That was perfect. She went to the freezer and grabbed a juice. When she turned around, he was behind her, so close that she almost spilled the contents of the bottle.

He laughed, looked at her hand and said:

- That taste is delicious; I will get one too.

This time she smiled back and gave him the go ahead. She was trembling so much that her jaws were clenched.

- Pull yourself together, Rosana; Don't do anything silly now - she thought without taking her eyes off him.

- Too bad you do not have my favorite - she said, trying to put a casual tone in her voice - I really like pears.

He lit up the room with his fantastic smile and lifted the bottle:

- It is my favorite too, but as a second choice I will take the grape. So, here's to coincidences!

At that moment he gave her a different look; it was softly profound and seemed to go straight to Rosana's soul. It expressed an affection that warmed her heart. And slowly, Rosana calmed down and felt more confident and secure. She wanted to snuggle into his chest, to hug him...

Instead, she spoke:

- This is a very good area! I hope to find the property I need. Do you know this area well? - she asked in a natural way, but secretly laughing because she did not know where she got the idea.

- I am sorry, but I do not usually talk to strangers - he replied, looking annoyed.

- Huh? - startled Rosana. But when she saw the look on his face, she understood the joke and they both laughed.

- Rosana, nice to meet you!

- Walmir, nice to meet you too! And now to answer your question with another question: residential property?

- No. I am looking for a commercial room, not too big to set up my office, and I like it here, but I have not been able to see for myself if it has what I am looking for.

- I think I can help you. My office is in the building next door, and I know there are some rooms for rent. If you like, I can accompany you there. Rosana could not believe what was happening. She was there with him, she knew his name, where he worked... It was unbelievable!

- Please, Walmir, I do not want to get in your way.

- Not at all; if I have offered, it is because I have time available. Do not worry, all right!

- My car is outside, and I do not think I locked it. I will go there and then we will look at the rooms.

- I will wait for you here. Rosana left feeling like she was floating. She did not have any plans now. She would just let things happen.

- What an idea to say I am looking for a room... I want to see you get out of this, Mrs. Rosana! - she thought as she took a deep breath. When she saw him leave the store, she went to meet him, and they walked together to the building where she had lost sight of him a month earlier. They stayed together for almost two hours. They went through a few rooms, and he showed a real interest in helping her; she could see that he did it with respect, without any hint of any other intention behind it. He then invited her to visit his office, where she was greeted by a small group of staff, all very friendly and polite, which delighted her. When they said goodbye, Rosana had already discovered a very important fact about him, perhaps the most important, but she did not want to think about it now.

- Walmir, thank you so much. You were very kind to help me. I really liked that room on the second floor. I am going to take my time and maybe I will get it.

- The best way to thank me will be to resolve this issue and achieve great success in your venture - Walmir replied, taking Rosana's hand in his.

She walked to her car feeling immensely happy; as she passed the store, she waved to the cashier and drove off. She drove without knowing where she was going. She just wanted to walk aimlessly, feel the cool breeze on her face, listen to her favorite music. She looked around and had the impression that everything was more beautiful. The colors were brighter, the city more charming than ever. She did not want to see anyone, she did not want to talk, she just wanted to keep the feeling caused by recent events inside her for as long as possible.

It was almost late afternoon when she returned home. She did not bother unpacking her suitcase. She poured herself a glass of milk and went to her room, where she sat quietly, just thinking for a few hours.

It was already dark when she took a shower and decided to go out again. She went to the bookstore she used to frequent; it was a large store with an internet café attached and it was open 24 hours a day. When she arrived, she looked for religious books, a section she did not usually pass through. When she saw the spiritualist books, one immediately caught her eye: The Spirits' Book, by Allan Kardec. It dealt with the immortality of the soul, the nature of spirits, how they related to man and moral laws. She was sure that this was what she was looking for. She paid for the book and went to sit in the café, ordering a hot chocolate.

After checking the contents of the book through the index, she picked up her cell phone:

- Hi Nanda, sorry about the time, but I really wanted to talk to you! Fernanda loved hearing Rosana's voice.

- I was worried you had not called yet. How are you? Where are you? Tell me, friend, how are you? - she said, anxious for news.

- Calm down, everything's fine. Believe me, just fine. And I am in São Paulo. I have given up on leaving the city! - she replied serenely. Fernanda was completely confused.

- No, something is wrong. This change of plans, you calling me at this hour, I do not know! - and continued without giving Rosana a chance to say anything - Gilberto is here with me. I am going to ask him to take me to your house and there is no point in you disagreeing.

- I am not at home, but given your determination, I think I will go there now, before you get your face in the door - she replied, laughing. Fernanda was angry with Rosana:

- I do not know what to do! I am worried sick, and you are laughing at me!

- I am sorry, but I didn't mean to mock your care for me. But are you going out now? Gilberto will not like it.

- Prepare the sofa bed in the other room and I will sleep at your place tonight. Tomorrow is Saturday and we can talk all night. Gilberto will understand. Fernanda had already spoken to her boyfriend about her concern for Rosana but had not gone into detail about the reasons. She just said that Rosana seemed to be on the verge of exhaustion. That night Gilberto did not create any problems. Despite his reserved style, he had good feelings and admired the friendship and affection that existed between the two. He took Fernanda to Rosana's house. They arranged for him to pick her up the next day, around lunchtime. When they met, Fernanda marveled at Rosana's appearance. She looked beautiful and serene, very different from the distressed image of recent times. She told her everything that had happened that day, and showing her the book she had bought, she concluded:

- Now I know you were right! There is something very strong that connects me to Walmir, and it is something that comes from another life, I am not sure. But I will try to understand. Fernanda was dazzled by the story she had just heard and could not say anything. Rosana continued:

- There is just one more thing I have not told you yet: he is married! Fernanda was stunned and finally spoke up:

- Rosana, that is crazy! What now?

- And there is more: do you know why it took me a month to find him again? Because he got married two days after the storm. Having said that, Rosana got up and went to get a cigarette. She sat down again and confessed, now expressing her sadness in words:

- What I feel is very confusing. At the same time as being immensely happy for the opportunity to meet him, I feel as if a knife has been plunged into my chest when I think that he has just got married. I would never have the courage to get involved with a married man.

- And Roberto? How does he look in all this?

Rosana did not hesitate:

- I am going to end my relationship. He does not deserve me cheating on him. I do not know what will happen from now on, but the mere fact of having someone else in my thoughts is reason enough for me not to be able to go on with Roberto.

- But he is going to suffer a lot, you know that Rosana... - Fernanda pondered.

- I know, my friend, and it hurts me too much. Despite everything that is happening, I have strong feelings for him and a lot of affection. And I know that if I betray him, he will suffer even more. Fernanda nodded silently. But she was really apprehensive about all this.

-Are you not scared, Rosana?

- I am... sometimes! But when I think of Walmir, I am sure that something very good is yet to happen, and I cannot avoid the path that is opening for me.

- I am going to see Roberto tomorrow. I want to resolve this with him as soon as possible. It will be better for both of us. They talked a lot during the night and went to bed very late, overcome by tiredness.

Chapter 5

The morning dawned and Rosana woke up worrying about the conversation she would have with Roberto. She knew how difficult it would be and how much he would suffer. But her mind was made up and she was sure it was the only thing to do. She thought of Fernanda's words about feeling afraid... She was ending a serious relationship, a beautiful story, to venture down unknown paths that could be very painful. But a single thought of Walmir was enough to dispel all her fears.

Fernanda said goodbye to Rosana and left with Gilberto but still advised her friend to think long and hard before talking to Roberto. Rosana promised to think about it, but she knew her mind was made up.

Around lunchtime she phoned him, who took the call with surprise when she said she was in São Paulo and would like to meet him for lunch. Rosana asked him to come to her house.

Roberto, who in recent times had already experienced moments of doubt about the stability of his relationship with Rosana, now felt that something very serious was happening. He jumped the gun and arrived a little early for the meeting. He was anxious, worried, and when he saw his girlfriend's serious expression, he felt an enormous weight on his head.

Rosana was very nervous, which made her get straight to the point, without beating about the bush, perhaps in the hope of getting out of this situation soon.

- Roberto, what I must tell you is very serious, and I want you to know that I thought a lot about it before I made this decision. We cannot go on together...

- Saying this, she kept quiet, waiting for him to react.

But he did not say anything. He just looked at her without saying a word and with an expression that Rosana could not define. She felt disconcerted and continued:

-It is very important to me that you know that you have always made me very happy! You are a wonderful man and there is nothing you have done to make me do this. I am going through a time of a lot of doubt about my life, including my career, and I cannot stand next to you and put you in the middle of my inner conflict. I need to be alone to decide what I want to do. I have enormous affection for you and because I respect you so much, I do not want to involve you in this - she concluded, getting up and lighting a cigarette.

Roberto lowered his head and thought... he got up too and went to the window. Rosana became increasingly distressed by his silence. Until he spoke a few minutes later:

- You are with someone, aren't you? - he said, feeling a lump in his throat.

Rosana regretted having to lie, but she knew she could not tell the truth; it would be too difficult for anyone to understand, and for him even more so.

- I would never betray you. No, I do not have anyone... - she answered without being able to look directly at him.

- I do not understand... I know you have been tired lately; we even talked about your vacation... we all have problems, love, I can try to help you, we can solve this together. Why such a radical attitude? - he was confused and did not believe his own arguments. Rosana put out her cigarette with a trembling hand.

- My God, I cannot make him understand and it's going to be difficult for him to accept my decision without at least a coherent reason - she thought nervously. She walked to the kitchen and returned with some water. He watched her in silence. It was then that she turned to him with great discouragement:

- I do not know what to tell you... I have already said that it is my problem, doubts, questions that I must resolve. I want to change my life and... He interrupted her abruptly:

- And I am not part of your plans for this new life. So that is it? That is, it? So many years together, and now goodbye, it is over... - Roberto was starting to lose control. He felt resentment and hurt. Rosana was irritated by his tone of voice.

- What more do you want me to say? There are many reasons why a relationship ends. And when it does, we cannot help it. I am sure anyone would love to love just once in their life, start a family, stay in the same job until they reach the top of their career, have no problems, have no doubts... But that is not how it works! I did not want to hurt you, but why does it always have to be this way? To avoid hurting you, I will have to hurt myself. Roberto looked at her angrily:

- EGOIST! That is what you are being. You are not giving me a chance...

- And what chance are you giving me? - she was also getting out of control.

- You are pressuring me to carry on with a life together that will not work... at least not now!

- Ah! - Roberto said sarcastically – it is not going to work out now, and you want me to wait for you to resolve your conflicts and stand by with open arms to welcome you if you decide to come back. He concluded by turning his back on her. Suddenly Rosana calmed down, lit a cigarette and addressed him firmly:

- It is your choice. Everyone must be responsible for their decisions. If I regret my decision, want to come back and you do not accept me, I will have to bear the consequences, and I cannot blame you for anything. I do not want you to wait for me... I am just asking you to understand that I am being as honest as possible with you and that it also hurts me to make you suffer. It would be worse if I deceived you about my feelings, making you think that everything is fine between us when that is not the truth - she took a deep breath and continued:

- Please, everything is already very difficult. Roberto was upset.

- Rosana, you will regret this! And I will not be around when it happens, you can be sure of that - he said and left, slamming the door. Stunned, Rosana stood still, unable to believe it had happened like that. They had had a fight; he had left hating her; she had been disappointed by his lack of understanding... so different from what she had imagined. She knew it would be a complicated conversation, but not one that would go that far. You can live with someone for years and never imagine what they are capable of. Human beings really are unpredictable. She was exhausted and fell back on the sofa, where she spent some time trying to recover. She felt guilty, irresponsible. What was she doing with her life? At that moment, Walmir's image came back to her mind... and she smiled. She pulled out a pillow and pressed it against her chest, feeling her heart beat faster. The thought of Walmir was enough to make everything else lose its importance. A hurricane of sensations and feelings formed inside Rosana. She was in love with him, there was no denying it; on the other hand, why had she reacted like that when she first saw him? And if it was against her principles to get involved with a married man, why hadn't she simply ignored everything and carried on with her life as usual? Would she have the courage to keep in touch with him? He was newly married, and it was clear that he was not looking for any adventure at the beginning of their married life; she did not want that either. He was going through that phase of infatuation and passion, and Rosana was sure to get hurt. But she thought about it all, and even so, she could not give up the path she had taken. Her body shuddered... she felt afraid.

She got up and went to the shower. She was going to use every moment of her vacation to let things happen. She would live each day without worrying about the future.

In the middle of the afternoon, Rosana went out to see the office in the building where Walmir had his office. It was just a pretext to meet him. As she passed through the main lobby, she bumped into Daniel, Walmir's employee. They chatted for a while, and she learned that Walmir would not be returning to the office that afternoon. When they said goodbye, Rosana disguised herself and left the building without even going upstairs to see the room. She was disappointed not to have found him.

- Patience... it was just one day! - she thought, trying to come to terms with it. She went straight to the supermarket to buy a few things that were missing from home.

The next few days were a time of recollection for Rosana. She spent most of her time at home, reading and resting, only going out to take care of things that could not be helped. And on each of these outings, she always passed close to Walmir's work. On two occasions she even saw him in the street, but she kept her distance, just watching. And that was enough to make her feel happy!

After a week, Rosana showed up at the office, and Fernanda was delighted with her arrival, but she could not imagine what had prompted her friend to show up at the company in the middle of her vacation.

Rosana called Fernanda in for a coffee and explained that she needed to talk to João Paulo, and that she would tell her everything after the meeting. Fernanda was intrigued and curious, but nothing surprised her more about Rosana's attitudes since she had met Walmir.

An hour later, Rosana left João Paulo's office visibly calm. He accompanied her, but wore a contrite expression, even a little sad. He kissed her on the cheek, wished her luck and success and then left.

Fernanda stared at her in amazement, and all it took was a sign for her to follow Rosana into her office.

- I cannot stand it anymore! What is going on?

- Fernanda, today a part of my life is definitively over, and you can be sure that from now on I will be much happier. Fernanda noticed a new glow lighting up Rosana's smile.

- I have just resigned! - said Rosana with contagious joy.

- I cannot believe it! Now what? What are you going to do? - Fernanda asked, concluding that Rosana could still surprise her much more than she had imagined.

- I am going to set up my own business consultancy company. I have always had this dream and now I have worked up the courage to make it come true. João Paulo has come to an agreement with me, and he is going to fire me so that I can get the money for my employment rights. Together with my savings from all these years, I can set up the office and I will still have time off until the business starts to pay off. A shadow of concern appeared on Fernanda's face, and it did not go unnoticed by Rosana, who hugged her friend:

- Nanda, I am happy, very happy, and I would like you to share this feeling with me. Take that wrinkle out of your forehead and wish me success too.

-Rosana, you know how much I love you and I am very much looking forward to your happiness. Of course I worry, but you look so radiant, so beautiful...What can I say? I will always be by your side, supporting you and helping you in any way I can. I know you are doing the best for yourself. I would just like to ask you one thing: where is your new office going to be? - Fernanda added.

-Would you like to guess? - Rosana replied, looking childish. They both started laughing.

-You really are amazing! When I grow up, I want to be just like you - said Fernanda as she helped Rosana pack her things. The next day, Rosana signed the lease for the office and when she picked up the keys, she felt strong, confident, as if she could conquer the world. She thought of Walmir, and a great tenderness came over her. Her eyes filled with tears, which she tried to disguise. Again, there was that tightness in her chest, that pain she had not felt for some time. This feeling made her very confused, and Rosana tried to get away from it and not think about anything.

Rosana's parents received the news of their daughter's new plans with admiration and joy. They had long thought that Rosana deserved to have her own business and considered that she had the necessary skills to achieve success. They had a celebratory dinner and did not touch on the subject of Rosana and Roberto's break up. They believed she was responsible and did not like to interfere in her private life unless she asked for help.

Rosana's life changed completely. Everything she did was with passion and joy. She felt motivated, with a renewed will to live. It was then that she realized that, until she met Walmir, her life had been too quiet, too straightforward and without passion! In her relationship with Roberto, everything was as if they had been married for years, even though they lived separately. At work, she achieved her goals, she was respected, but something was missing. And now she knew what it was: passion, drive, will... that feeling that makes you see the world in the most vibrant colors, that makes your eyes always seem to light up, that fills your heart with love; love of life, of everything, of everyone!

Walmir was in his office when his secretary told him he had a visitor. He welcomed Rosana with joy. After greeting each other with a kiss on the cheek, she took his hand and gave him the keys to his new office. He smiled, showing real satisfaction, and then said:

- That is great! It all worked out. Now we will be neighbors, how nice!

- I am very excited about the news. I want to set everything up as quickly as possible, roll up my sleeves and get to work. And once again you will be involved, only now I will be your client. Do you agree? Walmir was an architect and when he graduated, he opened an interior design company.

- Do you want one of our projects? - he asked flattered.

- Only if you take care of everything yourself, after all, I owe it to you to get my new office. Walmir was visibly embarrassed:

- Imagine... you do not owe me anything! It was only in my power to help, and I was happy to do it.

- So, do you accept the job? - asked Rosana, certain that the answer would be yes.

- How about we start now? - Walmir enthused, then picked up the intercom and ordered two coffees, only to be interrupted by Rosana:

- Would you like something else to drink? - saying this, she took two bottles of pear juice out of a bag, still cold.

- I thought you would accept my request, and we would celebrate - she winked at him. Walmir was charmed by her manner, and they ended up spending hours discussing the design of the new office. From then on, they met every day. Rosana spent most of her time in the office and they went out together a few times to choose materials, decorative pieces, furniture, etc. She often spoke to Fernanda and apologized for not having enough time to spend together. Fernanda was thrilled with every new development and promised to go and see her friend's new premises as soon as possible. Rosana seemed to be living in a dream. Everything was wonderful.

Walmir treated her with affection and respect. At no time was there any hint of anything other than friendship between them. He was very intelligent, had a fantastic sense of humor and a great presence of mind. And as if that were possible, the more Rosana looked at him, the more she found him handsome and charming. Sometimes she thought that none of it was real... after all, there is no such thing as perfect. But he was perfect!

No matter how hard she looked, she could not find a single flaw in Walmir.

Only two things intrigued Rosana: one was that he never talked about marriage or his wife. And the other was the way he looked at her at times. She had the distinct impression that he wanted to say something or ask a question. At these times, she noticed a certain enigma in Walmir's gaze, which made her curious and skeptical.

Chapter 6

The office was finally ready, and Rosana arranged a small gathering there to celebrate.

She called only her parents, Fernanda and Gilberto, a few friends and, of course, Walmir and his team.

Rosana arranged a small buffet with canapés, champagne and wine.

Everyone praised the tasteful decoration of the space, and Rosana proudly introduced Walmir, which soon caught the attention of her parents, who, despite realizing her excitement, kept a low profile and said nothing. Rosana's mother was delighted with him too and secretly began to hope that he was her daughter's new boyfriend, until she noticed the wedding ring he was wearing. If that were the case, she would talk to Rosana another time. In no way did she approve of her daughter getting involved with a married man.

But the big event of the evening, especially for Rosana and Fernanda, was Gilberto's behavior. They were impressed by how he had identified with Walmir, and the two of them spent most of the evening talking about the most diverse subjects. The stern and withdrawn Gilberto gave way to a cheerful, fun and friendly man.

The evening went wonderfully, and as soon as Rosana's parents said goodbye, the other guests left too, leaving only Fernanda, Gilberto, Walmir and Rosana.

When everything was tidied up, Gilberto said:

- Rosana, it is getting a bit late. Fernanda and I will accompany you home - a decision that met with Fernanda's full approval.

Walmir intervened:

- You do not have to worry, I can do it. Rosana's house is on the way to mine. It would be my pleasure!

Rosana looked at Fernanda pleadingly, almost out of breath.

-Well, love, if Walmir does not mind, it is just as well. We will take the opportunity to go to the video store and pick up a DVD, how about that? - said Fernanda, giving Gilberto a tender kiss on the cheek. All settled, the four of them said goodbye; Rosana went with Walmir to the garage where the two cars were and headed for her house. When they arrived, Rosana did not know what to do. All she wanted to do was invite him upstairs for a while and she plucked up the courage:

- Walmir, I do not know how to thank you for everything. Have you seen how many compliments you have received for the work you have done? It really is spectacular!

- When you do what you love, the result is always positive. And I try to act like that in every aspect of my life. Of course, in certain situations we must give up some things if we want to cause harm to someone else. But even when I have to do that, I try to see it as a benefit for myself, as growth and learning. This helps to ease any suffering - he concluded with a smile. Rosana was mesmerized and could listen to him talk all night.

- It is true, you are right! But what about when the suffering we cause is in ourselves?

- That is what I said: when a situation is unavoidable, we have three options: keep dwelling on the mistake, sit back and mourn, or try to find a new path and understand the reasons that led to it. I usually take the third option.

- So, you must be a completely fulfilled person - said Rosana, trying to get to know him better.

Walmir laughed and nodded negatively:

- No, Rosana; it's not like that. Of course, I have my frustrations and conflicts, but I always try to be happy and radiate that happiness wherever I can. When I feel sad or down about something, I dig deep to find the "why". I do not tend to run away from problems as many people do. And when I have any doubts, I always wait for the right moment to resolve the issue.

When he said this, Rosana noticed again that strange look he gave her from time to time. And this time, she felt that there was a veiled communication going on between them, which neither of them could quite understand.

She felt embarrassed and tried to get out of the mood:

- Would you not like to come upstairs? The conversation is so delicious...

- I would love to, Rosana, but I really must go. Maybe another time. I like it when we talk and this time, we have spent sorting out the project has been really fun and enjoyable, hasn't it?

- I loved it too! - agreed Rosana, disguising her disappointment at having to let him go. Walmir kissed her on the cheek and left. Rosana went home feeling drunk with happiness. She could not imagine what would happen from then on, but at that moment all she wanted to think about was him and all the moments they had spent together. The days went by, and Rosana began to hire her team, which at first would be small, just the essential staff. Then she had an idea that at first seemed absurd, but she thought it was worth the risk. He called Fernanda:

- Hi Nanda, It's me, what is up?

- Rosana, I miss you! I'm fine. You are on the go, aren't you? A lot of work?

- Not yet, I am in the structuring phase, and you know how it is, only then does it get off the ground. I need to talk to you; when can we meet?

- Today if you like. It is a pretty quiet day around here, even my new boss has not come in. I can take some time off in the afternoon. Does that suit you?

- Perfect then. How about we meet at that café around half past three?

- I will be there. Any big, good news?

- Maybe, I cannot say yet.

- See you later then. Rosana spent all morning interviewing candidates for the positions available in her company. She did not even go out for lunch. She bought a sandwich and ate it in her office. She kept thinking about Walmir and missed him terribly. She had not seen him for a few days, and heard that he had won several new projects, which made her feel happy for him.

After the night they went to his house together, Rosana thought their relationship would take another turn... but nothing happened. Even so, she did not let it get her down. She had already achieved a lot: she worked close to him, she got his friendship, they talked whenever possible. But the situation left her very confused. She was lost in thought when there was a soft knock on the door:

- Can I bother my best ex-client? - Walmir asked with his unique smile.

If Rosana had not finished her sandwich, she would certainly have choked, so happy was she to see him.

- Hi, Walmir. What a nice surprise.

- I am just stopping by to ask you a question: do you like reading?

- Wow, I love it!

- What genre?

- Any genre. I am a bookworm, really. Why is that?

- I have just read a book that I loved, and I thought I would recommend it to you. It is called "O Matuto" by Zíbia Gasparetto. He turned and picked up a small gift package he had left in the anteroom.

- For you, Rosana. I am sure you will love it. We will talk about it later and you can tell me what you thought. Rosana did not know what to say and was visibly moved. She held the book as if it were her greatest treasure. After lunch, Rosana stayed in her living room reading and only stopped when it was time to meet Fernanda.

-So, Rosana, what is new? - Fernanda asked, expecting anything but what she heard from Rosana.

- Nanda, I am going to be very direct: do you want to come and work with me? Fernanda was surprised and before she could answer anything, Rosana continued a little anxiously:

- I know you like your job, and you are doing well at the firm, and I will not be able to pay you much more, but I want you not as a secretary, but as my assistant for customer service. You know everything about our work, you have experience, and we have always made a great pair. Of course, where you are, you may have the chance to grow faster, so do not hesitate to refuse my offer. Fernanda smiled and did not wait for Rosana to say anything else:

- Rosana, if you did not invite me, I would invite myself. I have always thought about it, but I was waiting for you to take the initiative. The two shook hands and toasted happily. Everything was going so well for Rosana that she could not believe it. The only thing left to see was what direction her relationship with Walmir would take. Was that gift just a gesture of friendship or was there something more behind it? And how was his marriage going? He remained secretive about it, and she would never touch the subject. Gilberto was not surprised by the news that Fernanda was going to work with Rosana and was happy for her. He was very excited about his work, getting new students and starting to make real plans to set up his own gym. It seemed that a new phase in everyone's life was beginning and really changing for the better. Rosana read the book she had gotten from Walmir with great interest and soon reached the end. The story was about betrayal, settling scores and reincarnation. At times, she read the book she had bought trying to find answers to her doubts. Rosana felt that life was putting her in situations in which she had to make important choices and seek understanding for the events, and she remembered Walmir's words about learning and growth. She began to think about her life since she was a teenager and saw how much she had changed. She had always been a very cheerful and active young woman. She loved sports and took part in official teams at the schools she attended. She had a particular love of music and learned to play the piano. Her interest in the arts also included painting, which she began to learn but stopped. But after a certain period at university, she gradually abandoned her hobbies and when she started dating, she put everything aside and started living for work and for Roberto.

The exact opposite happened with Walmir. He brought back to her the Rosana of years ago, with more zest for life, a desire to make up for lost time and resume the activities that were so good for her. She felt more beautiful, really enjoying life.

Only one thing still shook her: that deep sadness she felt at times when she thought of Walmir. It was a very strong feeling, an almost unbearable pain, and she invariably cried. When she felt it, she always tried to distract her thoughts and see it as a fear of not being able to win his love. But even though she did not want to admit it, she knew that there was something else going on that she could not define.

Fernanda and Rosana were getting their first clients and business was going very well. Every new contract was a new lease of life.

One afternoon, Gilberto showed up at Fernanda's office by surprise. They chatted for a while, went downstairs for a snack and when they returned, Gilberto said goodbye and went to visit Walmir. A great friendship began to develop between the two, but Gilberto didn't tell Fernanda much about what they talked about, saying only that they chatted about various subjects.

One evening, when picking Fernanda up from work, Gilberto said:

- Nanda, what do you think about visiting us at a prayer meeting? Fernanda was surprised by the question. Gilberto had never shown any deep interest in any religion, and that invitation was surprising.

- My love, I never imagined hearing such an invitation from you - Fernanda replied, caressing her boyfriend's face.

- Where did this idea come from?

- Sometimes we are not interested in certain subjects, simply because we do not know about them. I have been talking about it and I started to see a lot of sense in the Spiritist doctrine. And I would like to get to know it a bit more, that is all.

- Talking?...Walmir? - Fernanda asked, intrigued.

Gilberto smiled:

- Himself! You know, love, he is a very nice person, a serious guy with excellent character. He follows the Spiritist doctrine and has told me a lot of interesting things. And the funniest thing is that there are times when I feel as if I have known him for a long time. Fernanda was amazed by Gilberto's manner. Because of his withdrawn temperament, he had many acquaintances, but no particular friends. And now, it seemed, he had just found one.

- Walmir really is very special. Everyone likes him. Does he go to that meeting you want to meet?

- That is right! He did not even give me a formal invitation, he just mentioned the place and I wanted to go. Can I count on your company?

- Of course, Gilberto. When are we going?

- Tomorrow night. I will pick you up from work and we will go straight there; the meeting starts early.

- That is fine with me. Arriving home, Fernanda called Rosana to tell her about the latest developments. Rosana was very interested.

- Ah Nanda, would Gilberto mind if I came along? Fernanda was thoughtful and answered cautiously:

- I don't know Rosana... I don't know the place or how things work there. Would it not be better if you kept a low profile? Everything is going so well, let's take it easy. Rosana quickly assessed the situation and concluded that Fernanda could be right.

- And there's one more thing Rosana: he could be there with his wife. Can you imagine that? Rosana shuddered just imagining the situation.

- Okay, but do you promise to tell me everything in detail later? Fernanda laughed:

- You still look like a teenager, Rosana. But I will write everything down in a little notebook, so I do not forget anything. That night Rosana had a hard time sleeping. Her love for Walmir grew every day. Apart from his smile, what Rosana loved most about him was his gaze, which was intense and tender at the same time. He had an impressive strength and frankness. And his eyes were very beautiful, brown and slightly drawn, and they squinted when he laughed. As their friendship grew, Rosana also discovered that Walmir was a man of excellent character, hard-working and with a big heart. He had solid principles when it came to honesty and responsibility. They no longer spent much time together, but she saw him almost every day. On a few occasions, they crossed paths on the street, in the building garage, but only greeted each other from afar. There seemed to be an attraction between the two of them; several times she would see him passing by and just stare; then he would turn exactly where she was; when he saw her, he would smile and wave.

She did not want to create fantasies in her head, but she noticed that he was looking at her, thinking she was not noticing.

Rosana also gave fate a little help. As he usually kept to a certain routine, she managed to find him at snack time, when he went to the convenience store. She would laugh at herself when she walked in and pretend to be surprised to see him. And then she wondered if he had noticed that there was nothing casual about these encounters.

But she did not care. She wondered if she was being too inconsequential, too immature, but then wiped those thoughts from her mind, justifying it by saying that she was only fighting for her happiness.

She was not very proud of what she was doing, but she could not help it. She wanted that man more than anything in the world. He was the best person she had ever met in her life, the most handsome, the most perfect, and she would fight to achieve her goal.

Chapter 7

Rosana arrived at the office very early and looking terribly sleepless. She asked her secretary to cancel all the day's appointments and move them to other dates.

When Fernanda arrived and heard about the cancellations, she went straight to Rosana's office.

- What is wrong, friend? Wow, you look awful!

- I had a long night... only it was not terrible because I thought about Walmir all the time - replied Rosana between sips of coffee.

- This way you will be finished. Have you ever thought about him stopping by today?

- No kidding, Nanda; he cannot see me in this state - she said, tapping the table lightly to scare away the possibility.

- But apart from that, are you all right? I would like to stay here with you, but I will not be able to.

- Do not worry, I am fine, I am just very sleepy - she lit a cigarette. I just wanted to ask you a favor: can you see if Gilberto can stop by today? I am not going out; I want to stay here in my corner. He can come at any time that is best for him.

- All right, we will sort it out now - she picked up her cell phone and spoke to Gilberto.

- He said he would be here in the morning, but he could not say when.

- No problem; I will be here.

- I have to leave now. I will be back at lunchtime.

- Yes, you will. I will talk to you later. Fernanda was just leaving:

- NANDA... She turned around and Rosana just said with a smile:

- Thank you! Fernanda just winked and left. Rosana put on some music quietly and realized that whenever she thought of Walmir, she listened to the same CD, and one song in particular sounded like him. She cracked a smile and thought:

- We already have our love theme... only he does not know it!

Gilberto arrived early to meet Rosana.

- I am so glad you came, Gilberto.

- I came as soon as I could; what can I do for you?

- I need a personal trainer!

- Are you kidding?

- Why? Can I not want to take better care of myself? And who could I go to, if not the best professional I know in the field - she bowed to him.

Gilberto laughed! Then he asked, frowning:

- Have you stopped smoking? - and looked at the ashtray with some cigarette remains in it.

She grimaced:

- I just want you to help me get in shape, that is all!

- Step number one: quit this horrible habit.

- Are you going to give me a lesson or not?

- Are you going to stop smoking or not?

The two looked at each other as if they were about to start a duel. She gave in:

- I promise I will try.

- Just trying is too little - added Gilberto teasingly.

- Okay... I will do the impossible - said Rosana, giving in.

- Can I put the first lesson on for tomorrow? - asked Gilberto, opening the agenda. They worked out the details and changed the direction of the conversation. Rosana was tempted to ask about Walmir and the meeting. But remembering their budding friendship, she thought it best not to say anything. She and Gilberto talked as they had never done before. When he left, she closed herself in on her thoughts again. Everyone had changed so much in such a short space of time. Her break-up with Roberto had happened just a few months earlier, but for her, the life she had led then seemed much more distant.

She wondered about her recent actions and whether she was doing the right thing, but something told her that the wrong thing was not to follow her soul's desire. "And who could condemn her for loving so much?" - she asked herself - "it depends on what I would do in the name of that love" - she then answered, ending this inner dialog. And as Walmir said, she would have to bear the consequences of her choices. Everything was complicated at the moment, but she hoped that things would get back on track and she could be happy.

When she was seized by this thought, she felt that pain in her chest again.

She leaned back in her chair and asked her secretary not to disturb her except in the event of a catastrophe. She sat still listening to music and eventually fell asleep.

She lived in a rich old farmhouse. The windows were all closed, and Rosana found herself alone in the large, dimly lit living room, despite the fact that it was a clear day. Her hands clasped together showed a certain restlessness. She looked around for something. She walked towards another room, but before she could reach it, the huge door to the house opened, and rays of light invaded the entire room... and amid that intense light, he entered and came towards her. Suddenly her heart began to beat more calmly, and she breathed a sigh of relief. Walmir came closer, looked at her with eyes full of love and stroked Rosana's long hair. She placed her hands on his and held them lovingly. They spent a few moments just looking at each other and then he spoke almost in a whisper:

- Do you forgive me?

Tears began to stream down Rosana's face.

- My great love... how could I not forgive you? All I want is for us to be together... the rest does not matter!

- My life... my dear Innocence... I will never leave you. Rosana looked at him completely upset. INNOCENCE? NO! It was her, Rosana, who was there...

- Walmir, what is going on? It is me, ROSANA! Walmir did not even seem to hear what she was saying and kept looking at her passionately without realizing that she was completely upset. Rosana stirred in her chair and woke up startled. It took her a few minutes to get herself together; she got up, got some water and washed her face. She dried her face and looked in the mirror.

- What a horrible dream! - she thought worriedly. But she remembered everything in such detail that it seemed real. She was very impressed. That name kept popping into her head: "Innocence!" Was she really losing her mind? She sat down again and tried to analyze the situation rationally, but once again she got nowhere. Everything in her mind was a mess. She thought she would better go home, but before she left, she left a note for Fernanda with her secretary, asking her to call him as soon as she got back.

Gilberto and Fernanda arrived early for the meeting. Neither of them had any idea what they were going to find, but they soon felt at ease in that place full of peace and tranquility. They were greeted by a very friendly girl who took their names and led them into a large hall, where there were several chairs arranged in rows, carefully arranged. Some people were talking in very low tones, others were reading quietly in their chairs or praying in silence. After choosing their seats, they looked around to find Walmir, but did not see him. Naturally, they remained silent, each concentrating on their own thoughts. A short while later, with the hall almost full, a man accompanied by two ladies stood at the microphone at the front of the hall. He spoke a few words to open the meeting, said a prayer and began to read a passage from the Gospel. Gilberto and Fernanda, holding hands, were attentive to everything. After the reading, comments were made on the theme and then the lights went out, leaving only a few points of blue light on. There was a moment of relaxation and prayer and then the meeting was closed, with an invitation for everyone to take a glass of fluidized water before leaving.

They stood up and saw Walmir. They went over to him and when they were very close, a girl came up and took his hand. Fernanda felt cold! Walmir showed sincere joy at seeing them but was disconcerted when his gaze met Fernanda's.

- How nice of you to come! - he said, greeting Gilberto with a hug.

- I would like to introduce my wife, Cristina. This is Gilberto and Fernanda.

Gilberto greeted Cristina with a handshake, a gesture Fernanda repeated.

The four of them chatted, but as a good observer, Fernanda noticed that Cristina was not at ease and seemed to want to leave straight away. Walmir was uncomfortable with his wife's attitude and soon said goodbye.

On the way home, Fernanda and Gilberto exchanged ideas about the meeting and agreed that they were both feeling very good after everything they had heard. Those people radiated love, and it was contagious.

Fernanda was worried about Rosana. It would not be easy to tell her that she had met Walmir's wife.

As soon as she got home, she called her friend: Nanda, I am so glad it is you! I could not wait for you to call anymore. How was it

there?

- Oh Rosana, the place is wonderful. You leave feeling incredibly light. You will love it. Rosana did not want to show any disinterest in Fernanda's comments, but she could not resist:

- Was he there? Fernanda took a few seconds to answer:

- Yes... and he was not alone. This time the silence came from Rosana. She took a deep breath and asked:

- After all, what is she like?

- In what way?

- Everyone...

- I cannot say much, because we only met Walmir on the way out and we talked very little. But I can tell you one thing for sure: she is not nice at all. And she did not seem to like being there.

-And how were they two?

- Rosana, anything I say could be hasty judgment. But look, you are much prettier than her.

- Thank you for your words of comfort. I'd better not think about it, otherwise I will go mad.

- That is right, it is good for you. You need a good night's sleep; Gilberto told me about tomorrow's class.

- Yeah, I am excited. I will go from the gym straight to the office, okay?

- Then we will talk more. Have a good night and sleep well.

- You too. Rosana hung up visibly dejected.

- She really exists - she thought sadly. Until then, everything had seemed like a fantasy. It was as if Walmir's wife was an illusion, not part of the real world. Now it was different; Fernanda had met her, spoken to her... there was a face! Wasn't it time to give it all up and forget about Walmir? Why did this idea seem so difficult? And why did he often show feelings for her too? She had to do something; the situation could not go on like this. If she had to, she would speak frankly about her feelings with him. That was the only way to put an end to this suffering. She was determined. She was not going to wait any longer.

Chapter 8

A few weeks passed without Rosana having the courage to open her heart to Walmir. They saw each other a few times but talked very little. Fernanda continued to attend meetings with Gilberto; she invited Rosana to join them on several occasions, but to no avail.

Fernanda was noticing that Rosana's state of mind fluctuated a lot, and this made her worry about her friend. Gilberto also commented that in some classes, Rosana would glow with joy. In others, she was apathetic and discouraged.

They were both in the office, and Fernanda decided to have a serious chat with Rosana.

- So, you said you were going to talk to Walmir. Did you really give up?

- No, I haven't. I am just missing a good opportunity.

- We create opportunities, Rosana. Is that not just an excuse not to have this conversation?

-Nanda, what can I do? It seems that everything I think is wrong. I am in love with a married man, I have strange dreams about him, I feel that he has strong feelings for me too and then I realize that he acts towards me with the same politeness and kindness with which he treats everyone, in other words, nothing special. And I cannot get rid of that pain, that feeling of longing for him. But how can I miss something I have never experienced?

- There are many things we do not know. The important thing is to realize that this situation is not in your life by chance. We all have many trials during our lives, and we overcome them when we are able to accept the facts and learn from them.

- This is pure conformism, Nanda. Does that mean we should not fight for what we want?

- That's not it. But we must be aware of the steps we take on the way to achieving our goals. We cannot go around like a tank, driving over everything and everyone to get where we want to go.

- Are you suggesting that I forget about Walmir? Why? Because he is married?

- No, my friend, because I know that in other circumstances you would never get involved with a married man. I am just trying to draw your attention so that you do not live this moment irresponsibly. Surely the two of you met in such a special way for a very strong reason. You need to try to understand and assess whether your path is really with him. You do not even know for sure what is going on inside him. And do not run over the facts; everything happens at the right time, and the right time is not always the one we want, you know?

- So, you are contradicting yourself; first you say that we create the opportunity and then you say that we must wait for the right time.

- Rosana, it is not wrong to try to open your heart to Walmir, and I think you owe it to yourself. But if things do not turn out the way you expect, then you must accept the facts and understand the wisdom of life. God does nothing to make us unhappy. Our unhappiness comes from the way we face situations. I believe there is a very strong connection between you; the way you met, your dreams and the way you say he looks at you. You really need to sort this out so that you can go your separate ways, together or not.

- Together Fernanda! I cannot imagine it any other way. And thanks for your help, but I do not want to think about it now. I will talk to him, you bet. Fernanda realized that there was no point in insisting at that moment. She changed the subject.

- What about that book you agreed to lend me?

- Ah, it is in my car. Shall we go and get it? We will talk about it again later, Nanda. I promise I will think about everything you have told me. The two went to the garage and chatted animatedly on the way. As they were picking up the book, they heard the sound of another car. Fernanda spoke naturally:

-Look Rosana, it is Walmir. Suddenly, Rosana picked up a CD, threw the keys on the floor of the car, locked the door and slammed it. Everything happened so quickly that Fernanda was startled. When she saw Walmir's car approaching, she understood everything in seconds. She looked at Rosana, trying to hold back her laughter, and just said:

- You really are crazy!

Walmir pulled up next to them.

- Hello, how are my nicest neighbors?

Fernanda did not dare answer. She knew that Rosana had the text ready on the tip of her tongue. It was what she expected. She was right!

- Hi Walmir, everything is fine. Or at least everything was fine! - she said, looking bored.

- What happened? - Walmir asked, attentive as ever. Fernanda could hardly believe it: Rosana was a natural actress. She had to stop herself from laughing.

- Imagine that I came with Nanda to get some things from the car, and I ended up locking the door with the key inside. Annoying, but no big deal. Fernanda was just about to go upstairs to get my spare house key and call a cab. I quickly go up and get the other car key.

- No way. Take the house key and I will drive you there. There is no need to take a cab, Rosana.

Ten to zero for Rosana, Fernanda thought with amusement. Rosana could barely breathe, and at that moment she ran out of steam. Fernanda immediately intervened:

- I will go up and get your key, Rosana. Just a minute. She then left and took the elevator. Walmir made a maneuver and opened the door for Rosana to enter. Soon after, Fernanda returned and handed the key to Rosana, who only managed to reply that they would be back soon. Without Walmir noticing, Fernanda winked and waved goodbye. They had barely left the building and Walmir noticed the CD that Rosana was holding.

- What is that?

- Oh, I was going to take it to listen to in the office. It is by my favorite singer.

- Can I listen to it? Rosana felt her heart race. "I'm going to listen to our music alongside him!" - she thought radiantly.

- Can you put it on? - asked Walmir, who was paying attention to the traffic. Rosana tensed all her muscles so that he would not notice how shaky she was. The music began to play.

- You know, Rosana, I have been wanting to tell you something for a long time, but I am afraid you will think I am invading your life. She held her breath and smiled:

- Walmir, we are friends, aren't we?

- You know I think you are so different from when we first met. You are livelier, you have gained a different glow, you are prettier! Gilberto told me that you are taking the gym seriously.

- Wow, has it changed that much? - she asked a little awkwardly.

- I am sorry, but when I first met you, your eyes seemed covered in a mist, I cannot explain it. Now you seem happier. We do not talk much about our lives, do we?

- It's true... we have known each other for a while, and we do not really know much about each other. But you know, you are right. Back then I did not have control of my boat. I went wherever the tide took me. And I felt I was fine. I only realized it was not the life I wanted much later. That is when I decided to set up my company and change other things too.

- Were you with someone at the time?

- A relationship of a few years. But I couldn't take it any further...

- It is so hard to end a relationship, isn't it? Even when you are sure it is necessary to end it. Not everyone has the courage to make that decision. Responsibility in some situations speaks louder. Or the feeling that we are where we should be. I am not sure.

- I sometimes have the impression that events are beyond our control... and when that happens, we do what must be done.

- Rosana, when we lose control over our lives, we are bound to put our foot in it and end up hurting ourselves. That's not good. We must always be alert so that we do not act in a way that we might regret later.

-Walmir, has not a situation ever happened to you that you feel you cannot escape? Something you cannot avoid?

- Yes, it has.

- And what did you do?

- I followed my heart, but I did not leave reason aside. When we do not control our feelings, they take over. And that is disaster for sure.

- But who can live happily like that? Always controlling yourself, policing yourself... don't understand.

- Happiness is within everyone's reach. It does not always come as we plan, but you can be sure that if we look carefully around us, we will see a thousand reasons to feel happy every day. We can find happiness in the simplest things.

- Now, for example, I am glad we are here talking. Aren't you?

Rosana felt like kissing him, hugging him, telling him it was the happiest moment in recent times, but she stopped herself:

- Of course I am happy. In fact, I am in a very good phase of my life at the moment.

- What a beautiful song! Of the ones we have heard so far, that is the one I liked best!

She was amazed. It was their music that he liked the most. Such a coincidence was not possible.

- It is the one I like best too!

He looked at her and smiled.

- It is funny, Rosana, sometimes I get the impression that we know each other so well. I have always wanted to tell you that, but it might sound like a line - he concluded, laughing.

- I would not complain! - she smiled and could not believe she had said that.

He did not take her words seriously, and continued talking casually:

-One day we might find time to talk more. Have you noticed that we only talk in the midst of the daily rush? We never stop to talk leisurely. Maybe you will have dinner with me one day?

- Would you like me to cook dinner? And you can rest assured that I am not flirting with you. They both laughed happily, and he accepted the invitation. She held back the urge to ask about his wife. She did not want to think about anything, just that she was having the happiest time of her life. They arranged to leave together the next day and go to her house. When they got back to the office, she thanked him for the ride and asked:

- Ah Walmir, I don't even know what you like to eat.

- Rosana, do not worry about it. A salad is fine, if it is good for you too.

- Perfect! - she kissed him on the cheek and went into her office. She noticed that he was watching her, as he had done so many times before. Fernanda was waiting anxiously:

So, how did it go?

You will not believe it: we are going out together tomorrow night. Or rather, he is coming over.

Wow, what about his wife?

I do not know, he did not mention it. Maybe tomorrow I will find out more about it. Have you noticed that she never comes to the building?

- That is true, and she has not been at the meeting either. I think their marriage is a bit weird.

Especially as it is so recent. Strange indeed.

-Are you ready for this meeting? I am afraid you will get hurt.

Fernanda - said Rosana in a more serious tone - I cannot tell you what I am feeling apart from immense happiness, but even if tomorrow night is the only night of our lives... I am going to live it intensely. And you can be sure that you were right: everything happens in its own time. I am ready for whatever happens. Tell me something, Nanda: what does Gilberto already know about my story?

- Nothing, Rosana. I have never spoken to him about it.

- It is better this way. It is all very crazy, and I do not know if he would understand.

- Gilberto has changed a lot Rosana, have you noticed?

- Of course, he seems like a different person. We are even becoming real

my friends and I am happy about that.

- He loves you too, you can be sure of that. He gets worried

when he sees you in a bad way, but he is also embarrassed to say anything to you. Then he asks me, but I never go into details.

-He and Walmir are friends, so it is best that he does not know anything at all. I am sure Walmir does not mention it to him either. Fernanda agreed. Rosana was so anxious that she could not concentrate on anything. She talked to Fernanda, and they decided to schedule some visits to clients for the following morning. Rosana wanted to occupy herself as much as possible so that the time would pass quickly. In the afternoon, she would go to the supermarket to buy fresh vegetables for dinner and return to the office to meet Walmir. Then she changed her mind and called him to ask him to meet her straight at home. She wanted everything to be perfect!

Chapter 9

It was dusk and Walmir had called to say he was on his way. The salad was ready, the house was cozy, only the light from the living room lamp illuminated the room. Rosana was dressed simply and comfortably, her long brown hair loose and with discreet make-up.

Walmir was also very simple when it came to dressing; he usually wore jeans and a T-shirt or polo shirt outside his pants. Although he liked to show indifference when it came to dressing, he was very vain, and his clothes were of good quality and impeccable. Anywhere he went, he immediately attracted attention. He knew this, but he avoided affectations and acted discreetly, which added to his charm.

Rosana was lost in her thoughts when the doorman called to say he was coming up. She waited for him at the door, and when he arrived and looked at her, the world stopped for her. Nothing else existed, just that moment, just the two of them.

- Hi, beautiful - said Walmir, smiling.

- Hi - she replied, feeling herself blush.

- Come in and make yourself at home. What are you drinking?

- Will you join me for a whisky?

- Of course. Can you turn on the stereo while I serve? The CD's ready.

- Is that it? I would like to hear it.

- That is the one. The music was already playing when she returned to the living room with the glasses. Walmir raised his:

- Here is to tonight! After the toast, he continued:

- Do you remember our first toast, Rosana?

- Of course, I do - she smiled - it was with pear juice. And the second one too.

- It has already become a trademark. Walmir sat down on the sofa and Rosana in the armchair.

- Your apartment is very nice. You have very good taste. I do not think you even needed me to decorate your office.

- Do not be modest. Your work was perfect, and I would not know where to start.

- Do you not feel lonely sometimes?

- Yes, sometimes I do. But nothing that depresses me. I love reading and music, so I end up distracting myself.

- I meant... well... Do you not miss having someone to share your life with? Have you never thought about getting married?

Rosana sighed; how many things she wanted to say... but it was not time yet.

- That relationship I had and told you about the other day was almost a marriage, we just lived in separate houses.

- And what happened? Did you have a fight?

- No, or rather, in the end, yes. He did not take the break-up very well. And I could not be convincing when I talked about my reasons, and I think he felt betrayed.

- But you fell in love with someone else?

She hesitated a little but answered firmly:

- No, I just discovered that I did not love him. I was used to him, comfortable in the situation. A lot of people live like that, just going through life out of sheer habit. At the time, I discovered that I wanted more, that it was not fair to me or to him to carry on a relationship without real love.

- You had the courage to change, and I think it has done you a lot of good. As I said, when we first met, I thought you were a bit sad.

- After that decision, I rediscovered myself, I recovered a lot of lost things, and I am happy.

- What about your plans for the future?

- I do not have any. I just want to carry on with my work and live one day at a time. A good future is the result of a well-lived present, so I am concerned with doing my best today. What about you, Walmir? You have always spoken little about your life. When we met you were coming back from your honeymoon, weren't you?

- That is true. You do not know Cristina. Fernanda and Gilberto were with her at the meeting.

Rosana shivered. It was the first time she had heard him utter his wife's name, and now she would try to find out everything she could about it.

- Does she never come to visit you at the office?

- It is rare. Her work takes up too much of her time. And I think that is a good thing.

- You must still be on your honeymoon, right? It is always like this at the start of a marriage - she said with difficulty, trying to disguise her interest.

- It is not like that, Rosana - he replied with a melancholy air.

- I do not understand... you have been married for such a short time...

- We already lived together... and it was fine the way it was. But little by little, she started pressuring me to get married. I let myself get carried away until she convinced me. I did not take part in any of the preparations; she took care of everything quickly and on her own. The next thing I knew, I was married.

Rosana was astonished. And she felt guilty for being happy about what she had just heard.

- But do you not love her?

- Cristina is a good person, we get on well, but I think I got into the same situation as you... I got complacent. I am sure she likes me more than I like her. But now it is done. There is no going back.

- No?

- Remember I told you about responsibility? I should have acted before I got married. Now I feel I must try to build my family and live as well as possible. Rosana now felt extremely calm and a deep affection for him took hold of her.

- Funny... if I tell you something you promise not to get angry with me?

- Promise, go ahead.

- I have heard that you are a great conqueror, but I do not believe it. You are too sensitive, responsible, have a good character... I cannot see you as a Don Juan. Walmir replied with a laugh:

- I know I have this reputation, and it is even responsible for many of Cristina's bouts of jealousy. But you are right, I am not like that. There was a time when I really dated a lot, I was not attached to anyone. But deep down I always wanted to find that special person, with whom I could build a nice life. Walmir pointed to the empty glass and Rosana asked him to pour them another shot. They changed the subject and started talking about different things, each other's tastes, life stories, and the evening went by without them realizing it. The conversation was so pleasant that they even forgot to eat. Walmir had already gotten up and was changing CDs on his own, pouring whisky and making himself completely at home. Rosana was calm and happy and everything flowed naturally. That is when Walmir put "their" CD back on.

He sat down on the sofa and looked deeply into Rosana's eyes. And she realized that she could not help it any longer. Holding his gaze, she spoke softly:

- Walmir, there are some things I need to tell you, I cannot anymore, I do not want to hold back anymore...

Walmir could not take his eyes off hers and remained silent. She took a deep breath and continued:

- Do you remember the day we met for the first time?

He nodded and said:

- Of course, that was the day you were looking for an office to rent.

Her eyes seemed to light up:

- No, it was not that day.

He was puzzled by her answer:

- No? What do you mean?

- The first time we met was on the day of that big storm, remember? When the city almost came to a standstill?

He lowered his eyes, searching his memory of that day and looked at her again:

-Of course I remember. It was the day before my wedding. But I do not remember meeting you. Where was it?

- You went to the convenience store to buy something and then left. I was there.

- Yes, I remember... wait, I think I remember seeing you... sorry, but it is a bit of a vague memory... She was not hurt by it, and she stood her ground:

- I never forgot... so much so that I came back several times afterwards to see if I could find you again. He was really surprised and curious:

- So, you mean that day with the juice...was not a fluke? Do you want to tell me everything?

- I do... and I must, otherwise I will explode! No, it was not a coincidence. I looked for you for almost a month after the first time I saw you. On that day of the juice, I was leaving town, ready to forget him. I even thought I was going mad, that you did not really exist.

Walmir looked at her with such affection and admiration that she felt even more confident about continuing:

- And when I went into the store, sure that it would be the last time... you reappeared and everything changed.

- And that story about the office... that you were looking for a property...

- I made it up on the spot - she replied embarrassed.

Walmir laughed, got up to get water for them both, and on his way back he stopped in front of her, held out his hand and made her sit down next to him on the sofa.

- It seems there is a lot I do not know yet - Walmir said affectionately.

- Ouch - Rosana sighed.

- I like that - said Walmir, trying to put her at ease.

- I am dying of shame... but I am going to tell you everything... Rest assured that I will not be shocked if, when I am finished, you walk out of that door thinking I am completely crazy.

- Stop being silly, Rosana. Tell me everything... She calmly recounted what had happened, and he listened attentively, increasingly surprised and amazed. After listening to almost the whole story, he asked:

- What about all the times we meet at snack time... She put her hands over her face and nodded.

He laughed.

- You really are incredible. I could not even imagine... must not have been easy for you.

- It really was not; in fact, it is not. I still cannot believe I had the courage to come here and tell you how it really happened.

- Only Fernanda knows about it?

- Only... who else would understand a story like that...

- I understand... and I think it is fantastic. No one has ever acted like this towards me. Rosana stood up and picked up a folder full of drawings made only in pencil. She showed them to him one by one.

What are these drawings?

- Each one represents some situation I experienced with you; even the most banal encounters. They show how I felt.

- Wonderful...

- And there is a very important detail that I have not told you yet, a part of the story that has intrigued me and that was the reason for everything. You must think that what I felt was love at first sight, right?

- Something like this...

-It is just that I did not tell you exactly what happened when you came into the store. When I saw you, I did not feel in love or attracted. I got a big shock. I felt sick, dizzy, my chest hurt a lot, and I cried like a child. If I were to go by what I felt the first time I saw you, I would certainly never fall in love with you. In fact, I would run away.

- But was it that bad?

- It was an almost unbearable pain... something I had never experienced before. He became serious, confused and felt a strong tightening in his chest. His gaze now showed anguish. When he told Rosana what he was feeling, she replied:

- That is exactly what I often feel when I think of you. I cannot understand it. Walmir held her hand and stroked it. Rosana continued her story:

- And then there are the dreams...

- What dreams?

- I have dreamt several times that we were together, but not now. In a very distant time, perhaps in the eighteenth century. And you ask me for forgiveness, say you love me... and call me Innocence. And when I try to tell you that my name is Rosana, you do not seem to hear. Walmir felt an uncontrollable impulse and pulled her close to him, putting her between his arms. She did not put up any resistance, and they both remained cuddled on the sofa in silence for a few moments. He was the first to speak again:

- This could all sound crazy, but I do not see it that way. Now I understand that there really is something that connects us. I have often had the feeling that you were very important to me. I wanted to take care of you, to make you happy, and I did not understand what I was feeling. It was also something different for me from everything I knew. And I never broached the subject with you because I could not explain it. I thought it best to give it time. And now, I do not know what to think, I do not know what is going to happen... I am confused.

- Do you know what I think, Walmir? That this moment we are living here, now, will be the only one. It makes me suffer, it hurts me a lot, but it is as if I am aware that this is how it must be, it is a certainty that I do not know where it comes from.

He stroked Rosana's hair and felt that he wanted to stop right then. She gently touched his entire face...

- I want to memorize every detail of your face... she spoke with her eyes full of tears. His eyes glistened too.

She walked away and went into the kitchen, and he sat there looking at the drawings. When she returned, he was standing by the window. Their music began to play... she came closer and he said:

- That is the song, isn't it?

- Every time I heard it, I thought of you... He gently pulled her closer, held her face with both hands, looked deep into her eyes, and kissed her! A kiss full of love, of emotion that had been contained until then. Their hearts seemed to be beating to the same beat. Their bodies were so close together that they seemed to be one. As they kissed, they were tightly embraced. That kiss was not just a union of bodies; it was a union of souls. A moment of intense feeling. When their lips parted, she embraced him:

- Let me feel you... I know it will only be this once... she said this with tears streaming down her face.

- No, Rosana, we do not know anything... Everything that is happening is too strong... but I have my marriage...

She interrupted him:

-Do not say anything... we are confused... only this moment matters now.

They hugged again and stared out of the window at the city lights, quiet, just feeling the warmth of their bodies together. It was the middle of the night when he realized he had to go. Rosana did not ask him to stay. She accompanied him to the door, and they spoke very little. He went to call the elevator, and she just watched. When the elevator arrived, he opened the door and looked at her:

- I will talk to you tomorrow.

She just gave him a sweet smile. He let go of the door and walked back to her, holding her by the waist and kissing her again. Then he left. For a few moments she could not move. When she got inside, she went straight to the sofa where she had just been in his arms... closed her eyes and relived every second of that night.

Chapter 10

Walmir was leaving the garage when Rosana was arriving at the office. They did not greet each other; Walmir just looked at her tenderly and gave her a smile. She reciprocated.

Fernanda was anxious for news and arrived early.

- So, Rosana, tell me about last night.

- Fernanda... I don't even know what to say. He is wonderful, in every way. He is the man I will love all my life; you can be sure of that.

- Are you two together?

- No, we are not together... but... he kissed me.

- So? How did it go? Did he spend the night with you?

- Do you want to know if we made love? We did not. It was just a kiss. But it was the most beautiful, intense, loving kiss I have ever seen.

- I do not understand, Rosana. What is it going to be like now?

- I do not think it will be... and I think I am going to change everything in my life again. He is a person of integrity, who loves his wife and wants to take care of his family, his work.

- Did he tell you that?

- More or less. He is as confused as I am about everything that is going on, and we have not talked about the future.

Rosana began to cry. She knew she would not have another moment with him.

- Rosana, darling, what can I do for you? I so wish I had the power to take away this pain I know you are feeling...

-There is one thing you can do... take me to the meeting with you?

Fernanda felt her heart squeeze. She would do anything to help. She realized that the love Rosana felt for Walmir was greater and stronger than anything else and it would be difficult to overcome this situation.

That same evening, the two of them went to the meeting together. Gilberto had to teach one of his students at that time and could not accompany them.

Rosana prayed as she had never done before. In silence, she opened her anguished heart to God:

- My God, I know I have never been one to pray and I have never given anything to do with spirituality my whole life. But I am here now, with a broken heart, asking you for help. I do not think you approve of my attitudes these days and I know I have not been acting in accordance with your laws. But what do I do with the immense love I feel for this man? What do I do to understand everything that is happening? The other day I was told that the Lord does nothing to make us unhappy... So why am I going through all this? Why did I go to find the love of my life when I know I will not be able to be with him? Why has my life turned upside down like this? Help me God... help me find the answers. Tears streamed down her face. On the way out of the center, a lady approached them:

- Hello Fernanda, what did you think of today's topic?

- I really enjoyed it, Ms. Helena. I would like to introduce you to my friend Rosana.

- Pleased to meet you! I would like to invite you. Did you know, Fernanda, that I hold prayer meetings at home?

- No, I did not.

- I would like you to come to tomorrow's meeting... Fernanda and Rosana looked at each other and had the same feeling that this meeting would be important.

- Yes, we will. Just tell us the address and the time. Helena handed over the information on a small piece of paper and said goodbye. On the way back, Rosana and Fernanda were talking:

- How are you feeling?

- When we arrived, I was very sad, but now it seems that my heart has calmed down a bit.

- Rosana, you are going through a very big ordeal. And you have a lot to learn from it... you must be strong.

- It is not fair Nanda... I was in his arms... I can still feel the warmth of his body, the taste of his kiss... I feel like I am going to die without him.

- Do not even say that, Rosana. You need to be calm now, pray for serenity to understand the reasons for everything and, if necessary, resignation to accept God's designs. And you still do not know what is going to happen from now on.

- Today, when we met in the morning, he looked at me with such affection... but the expression on his face looked like goodbye.

- You need to wait for events to unfold and clarify with him what happened between you.

- Nanda, I do not know why, but I am going back to the office. I will drop you off at home and go there.

- But it is already late. It is after eight o'clock.

- No problem. And do not worry, I need to think.

- Call me if you need anything. When he passed the building's entrance, everything was empty. She took the elevator, but instead of going to her floor, she stopped on the floor of Walmir's office. She stood in the corridor, thinking... Suddenly she saw a light go on inside his office. Without thinking twice, she went in. Walmir was alone and was surprised by her arrival.

- Sorry, I saw the light on and thought it might be you. He looked at her seriously. She felt cold.

- It is all right. Did something happen? Rosana could hardly believe the way he was talking to her. She was totally disconcerted:

- Has anything happened? I think we need to talk... don't you?

- Yeah, maybe you are right... about yesterday. I think we made a terrible mistake and got carried away by fantasies, illusions, I am not sure. Maybe we overdid it with the booze.

- You wanted me as much as I wanted you. For a long time!

- What happened at your house was circumstantial... the music, the drink... we just got caught up in the mood. She could not have been listening to that. This man in front of her was not Walmir... not the one she knew. Insecurity began to give way to anger inside her heart.

- What are you saying? You know it was not like that. What about everything you told me about how you felt about me? Walmir just bowed his head without answering. This attitude made her even angrier:

- What do you want? For me to be angry with you?

- It is nothing like that. I just think we have embarked on a meaningless story... I do not believe there is anything more than an attraction between us. Those dreams of yours... everything you imagined... was just a creation of your mind... do not kid yourself.

- Ah, the great sage has spoken! Are you not the one who believes in a lot of things like reincarnation, past lives and whatever else... and now you think I am making it all up? You know that what is happening between us is no illusion - she said this with his eyes full of water.

At that moment she realized that Walmir had dropped the mask he had been hiding behind since she had arrived. The tenderness and affection returned to his gaze, and she felt like running into his arms. But neither of them moved. She sat down and felt that enormous weight pressing down on her chest. She spoke in a low, tired voice:

-You are scared... know I am right. You know that if we go through with this, we will not be able to separate anymore. I know that too. That is why we did not love each other last night... if we did, there would be no turning back.

He listened to her in silence... he did not have the courage to disagree because he knew deep down that she was right. She continued:

- I do not know why all this is happening, but I do know that before you I was lost in myself; I did not do the things I liked anymore, I lived a life that was not mine, and I let myself get carried away by that false happiness. When I met you, I was myself again, I had a zest for life, I liked myself more. I am not going to charge you for that now. I have you to thank. You brought me back to life. And now... I do not know what I am going to do if I must carry on without you.

- Rosana, I did not want to make you suffer... - Walmir said insecurely.

- Do not worry... I know you are suffering too, although you cannot admit it. You are not seeing... yet. I would better go. Walmir made a gesture to restrain her but controlled himself. She opened the door, turned to him and spoke confidently:

- I love you, with all the strength in me.

She left, leaving behind a great void.

Rosana was determined to learn something from all this. She could not go through so much happiness, then so much suffering, for nothing. She just wanted to understand.

The following evening, she went to the meeting with Fernanda. This time she asked Gilberto to let them go alone. There were about ten people in the house, and they all sat around a large table covered with a white tablecloth. Helena gave each participant a glass of water and opened the gospel. She thanked God for the opportunity to be together and began to read. After the reading, everyone commented on the text they had just heard and said a prayer. They were silent when a medium sitting opposite Rosana sighed, looked at her and spoke:

-Rosa, my dear flower, how it pains me to see you in so much pain. Rosana was startled. She squeezed Fernanda's hand and could hardly speak:

- My grandmother... only she called me Rosa flower! Grandma Olivia?

-My dear, God has allowed me this moment of happiness so that I could come and calm your heart! Listen carefully, my love. Do not harbor any resentment towards Pedro. He loves you very much and only wants your good. Rosana looked puzzled at Fernanda. Who was Pedro? What was she talking about? Fernanda motioned for her to continue listening. Her grandmother continued:

- You have always been a person of little faith, and you are suffering for lack of enlightenment. Now that you know that we have lived many lives, you should also know that we are not allowed to remember what we have been through. You cannot and should not know everything, as this could cause you sadness, shame or amazement and hinder your growth. We return to fleshly life to learn, reap the rewards and make up for mistakes. This is the path to our progressive improvement. In other circumstances, you and Peter loved each other very much. You were Innocence, a beautiful girl, the daughter of a wealthy coffee farmer. Pedro's family were friends of yours and you were inseparable from an early age. At that time, my daughter, education was very strict, and you were both still very young. Your father was concerned about your courtship and arranged your marriage with Pedro's father. But his father did not want his son to take on the responsibility of a family before graduating as a lawyer and they agreed that the wedding would take place in two years. Your father, my dear, fearing that you and Pedro, driven by love and youthful enthusiasm, would go too far in this courtship, decided to send you to a convent until the wedding date. Pedro was very sad about this, but he loved you so much that he swore that everything would work out and that time would pass quickly. You, more intemperate, said that you could not bear to be away from him, that you would rather die, and asked to run away together and get married in hiding. When you returned, everything would be done, and your families would have to accept it. Pedro had always been very responsible and tried to convince you that this would be crazy and could even harm you in the future, but it was to no avail. You were deeply disappointed in him and went to the convent believing that he did not really love you, even though until the last moment he said he would come and get you as soon as possible. Feeling totally disbelieved, you spent your days alone, not wanting contact with any of the other girls there. Longing and sorrow were eating away at his heart and little by little, you let the sadness take over your soul and body; you stopped eating, slept badly and did not want to know anything else. The nuns tried to give you all the care you needed, to get you to eat, but to no avail. You soon developed a serious lung disease, and your parents were called in. The disease developed so quickly that they took you back to the farm, but there was not much more they could do. You had given up on living! When Pedro went to see you, he no longer recognized you and a few days later you passed away. Pedro was desperate, he felt guilty, he thought about dying too, but he was a strong young man with faith, and he managed to overcome so much pain. And now he has come back to find you to make you want to live again and to make you believe that true love can survive anything. He has come back to help you mature, to develop your faith... he has come to teach you how to love! And he needs you too, my dear. Pedro today is Walmir... and he is very special. You have everything to find your way. Pray, my dear, and guard the love you feel for him carefully, because it is a very precious possession. I must go now. May God bless you and all our brothers and sisters here.

  The medium bowed her head and everything went quiet.

Rosana was crying, and Fernanda handed her a glass of fluidized water and everyone prayed for her, and she gradually calmed down.

Helena approached, took Rosana's hands in hers and said in an affectionate tone:

- My dear, you are going through a unique time. You will have to face it with courage and responsibility. You still have other trials to face, and your faith will sustain you. Pray and trust. We will always be by your side to support you - she looked at Fernanda and got her nod.

As they left, Rosana was very upset by the latest events.

- Nanda, do you think I should talk to Walmir about everything I found out today?

Fernanda thought for a moment and then replied:

- I do not know, Rosana, it is a very delicate situation. It seems that he feels a greater force connecting the two of you, but is it time to find out the truth? His perception was not as intense as yours, and maybe it is time to continue like this, without knowing the details. You are a free person; it is easier to change the course of your life. But what about him? He has a commitment, a family. Perhaps he would suffer more. You heard what your grandmother said that he came to teach you how to love, and it seems he succeeded. But there is still a long way to go, and now it is up to you to help make his heart peaceful. He suffered a lot in the past with your lack of trust, with your disbelief in his love... don't make him suffer now either.

- I think you are right... but I still want to have the chance to talk to him one more time. The two went home. Gilberto was waiting for Fernanda.

- My love, how was the meeting?

- Wonderful, Gilberto. Ms. Helena is a woman of great sensitivity and a big heart. And all the participants are wonderful people. Are we going together next week?

- Of course. And Rosana, how is she?

- Fine - she answered evasively.

- Fernanda, I know there is something serious going on with Rosana, but since you never mention it, I understand that you want to keep it private. Just tell me one thing: is not there anything I can do? I would like to help in some way.

- You have already helped a lot more than you know. Your lessons have helped Rosana to regain even more of her self-respect and your friendship has been invaluable to her. You cannot imagine how happy she was when you started to get closer. She always tells me that she no longer remembers that closed off and somewhat unfriendly Gilberto she used to know - she concluded, smiling.

- Wow, what an idea she had of me; I am glad she has changed - he replied, laughing.

- I am also glad that you are getting on so well. Meanwhile, Rosana had arrived home and went straight to the shower. She could not stop thinking about Walmir and what her life would be like from then on. She felt that she would not have the strength, that she could not bear to be without him. Then she remembered how she had behaved in the past and realized that she was about to make the same mistake, and everything that had happened between them would now be in vain. She had to fight and find the right path on her own. She loved him intensely, and would not do anything to harm him, ever! She did not think she could go on without him, and at that moment she began to pray and ask God for guidance and strength. The next day, while still at home, she decided to call Walmir.

- Hi... how are you?

Walmir was deeply upset. He felt that he had hurt her very much the last time they had talked, and he did not know how she was feeling now. And there was no way he could remain indifferent to her, even if he tried.

- Hi Rosana, I am fine and you?

- I am fine. I wanted to apologize for the way I spoke to you in your office. I got out of hand and was unfair. Walmir felt his heart squeeze. How he wanted to tell her how much he wanted her, that she was right about everything, that he would love to make love to her. Once again, he held back his feelings.

- Rosana, you do not have to apologize to me for anything. I was not right with you either. I did not want to hurt you for the world.

- You are going to be defensive about what I am about to say, but I know you are frightened by the idea of us getting even closer, and I can only say that you are right. It is best to keep the situation as it is. I will forget about you; you can be sure.

- We can be friends... - Walmir said, lacking conviction.

- Can I charge you in the future for what you have just said?

- What?

- That you will forget me.

- No, of course not. That is my problem now. But I am not going to do anything to compromise you or disrupt your life. I want you to be happy, with all my heart... and I think that one day we could be friends.

- I wish you the same... that is all that matters in our lives: that happiness.

After a short moment of silence, he said it again:

- Is that goodbye?

Rosana felt she could not speak any more:

- One day you will understand that we will never say goodbye... - and thought it best to end the conversation, which was already too painful for her.

- A kiss Walmir, stay with God and take good care of yourself.

- Rosana, take care of yourself too.

Rosana put the phone back on the hook and felt it was the end. She looked around, walked over to the window and slowly opened it. She took a deep breath of the morning air, looked out over the city and had the feeling that she did not belong anywhere...

Chapter 11

The day dawned and Rosana woke up with a sore body, the result of the stress she had been through. She felt melancholy and in no mood for anything. She looked in the mirror and saw nothing more than a shadow of the woman of a few months ago. She took a deep breath, trying to find the strength to carry on with her day. The phone snapped her out of her daze. Still hesitant, she answered.

- Hi Rosana, how are you? - Fernanda asked affectionately.

- I don't know... very tired. But I am going to react, although right now it seems impossible to do so.

- I am going to tell you something that might make you more awake; I am sure you will be surprised.

Rosana showed no immediate interest.

- João Paulo left the firm. He called me just now to tell me the news and asked if he could come and visit us. I promised to confirm as soon as possible.

This time the news made Rosana react:

- I can't believe it! What a thing! I always thought he would be the next director of the company. I wonder what happened?

- He did not go into details, but he was looking forward to meeting you. What do you say? We arranged something today... maybe in the afternoon. Work is always an excellent remedy for any ailment, and Rosana was very curious.

- Okay. Call him and try to arrange a meeting for after lunch. I will be much better by then, I am sure. Rosana took a quick shower and went to the beauty salon. She wanted to feel beautiful and lively and thought that this would be the best way. She called Gilberto to let him know that she could not go to the class and he did not ask any questions; he just reminded her how good the training was and that she should not get discouraged. When Rosana had finished doing her hair, she realized that her greatest beauty lay within. There was no point in improving her appearance if her spirit was sad. The change would have to be even greater. But at least she did not look so downcast.

She was entering the garage when she saw Walmir's car pulling away. She felt relieved: he had not seen her. Their meetings had become an embarrassing situation for her... or perhaps for both. It would be better to avoid them.

Fernanda was waiting for her and told her that João was on his way. He soon arrived. Everyone was happy to see him again, but Rosana and Fernanda were immediately interested to know what had happened.

- You can't imagine how that company is doing. Everything seems to have spiraled out of control, it is impossible to do a good job. Remember Adriano, that guy who started an internship? Well, he is nothing but a brat, a terrible bad character and an opportunist.

- You don't say? What has he done? - asked Rosana, dumbfounded.

- Instead of worrying about learning and doing his job, he started observing everyone, from the housekeeper to the director. He listened in on conversations and then, like someone who does not want anything, passed on to the director what he thought he should know, and appropriated ideas to make the boss think they were his. Only he is so naughty, he managed to do it without any of us noticing. The next thing we knew, he was being appointed the new general manager. Of course, nobody liked the appointment, but most of us had to accept it. But not me. I taught that bastard a lot of things, and I am not going to let him boss me around now.

- Anyway, that was it. I have resigned. And I am here to make myself available to you if you need anything. Maybe I can help you in some way. Rosana immediately had an idea but did not put it into words. They talked about the business and agreed to revisit the situation the following day. João Paulo left excited and confident that they would work together again.

- What do you think Rosana?

- Fernanda, I think life is really wise. João Paulo's arrival could not have been more opportune.

- I'm not sure I understand your idea, friend.

- Between us, the game can be open, Nanda; you know I do not have a mind for anything. I do not feel up to doing any work.

Fernanda interrupted her:

- Are you going to run away again? You tried it once and saw that it was not the way to go.

- I do not want to run away. But at the same time, I feel I can't be so close to Walmir. At least for a few days. It is very difficult to accept everything that is happening. Every time I see him, I want to run up to him and hug him and never let go. The desire I feel for him is so great that it feels like I am going to explode; sometimes I close my eyes, and I can feel his touch on my body. Maybe by moving away a little I will learn to manage my feelings better.

- I think you are starting to find the key to your peace now. I am sorry to say this, but we know you will not be able to forget him, but you will have to keep this feeling to yourself. Rosana did not know where to find the strength, but she had to fight to keep from falling into a deep depression.

- I still cannot quite understand all this. The things my grandmother said at the meeting... what is the point of learning to love and not being able to live it? What is the point of having knowledge that I will never be able to use again? I cannot have the man I love and at the same time know that I will not love anyone else...

- Who knows, maybe one day you will live that love?

- You say in another life, don't you? Because in this one I do not see how.

- With everything that happened in the past, you ended up acquiring responsibility with other people too, receiving new missions that you must fulfill. At that time, you used your free will to give up; you did not want to believe in your love, you did not have the courage or the faith. Everything has its time. Yours may not be now, but who knows, maybe you will be together forever?

- If it is in another life, it will not do me any good. I will not even remember... I want him here, now.

- There are many things we still need to learn. But you said yourself earlier that life is wise. Don't try to take the helm if you do not know what sea you are in. As my mother says: "When we do not know what to do, we should give it to God. He will certainly do better than us."

- I ask God to bring Walmir to me. I pray intensely every day.

- No, Rosana, do not ask for that. Ask God to protect you and give you the understanding to accept the direction life is taking. Ask to find happiness and wish Walmir the same from the bottom of your heart.

- I regret some of the things I say at times - said Rosana sullenly.

- But believe me, Nanda, I love him so much that his happiness is much more important than mine...

- Careful Ro, that is not how it is supposed to work. What you said shows imbalance, extreme feeling. And that can be dangerous. Your happiness is just as important as his. The love you have for Walmir is beautiful, I swear, I have never seen anything like it. But even the most beautiful love can become a cruel feeling if it gets out of control. Remember? Learning to love...

- You are right, Nanda. That is what I said about managing feelings. It is complicated, but I am aware that I now can learn how to handle myself better, to mature.

- You will find the right course, I am sure. And I think that after all this, you will be ready to love again.

- No, loving as I love Walmir will never be possible with someone else.

- There is someone in this world who needs you very much. When Fernanda said this, her face took on a different expression, as if she knew who she was talking about. Her gaze became distant, lost, vague...

- What are you talking about? Fernanda woke up from a kind of trance; she was confused:

- Huh? ...

- You have gone strange now, Nanda.

- I just meant that there may be someone who will awaken in you a feeling of affection and even love. I know it will not be the same as what you feel for Walmir, but who knows, maybe you will be happy with someone else.

- The present is already too complicated. Let's leave the future for later.

- What about João Paulo? What have you decided?

- Well, as I was saying, I think he has arrived at the right time. I want you to take over the company and make him your advisor. I will be available for any eventuality, but I need you to take over for the time being. Otherwise, our firm will be the shortest-lived in history.

- Are you sure about this, Rosana?

- Of course; I am sure it will be in great hands. I am not going to leave town like I did last time. I just want to get away from here for a while. When I arrived today, I saw Walmir leaving. That is not good for me. I am going to continue my classes with Gilberto and do what I had planned when I met Walmir again: I am going to look after myself. I am passing on the folder, my friend; now it is up to you. Call João Paulo and arrange what you think is best. I will follow everything from home, okay. I just do not want to come to the office.

- You can count on me. I will arrange everything. Thank you for your trust.

The two hugged and Rosana left. As she was getting into her car, Walmir appeared. He signaled for her to wait and approached her:

- Rosana... how nice to meet you.

She did not say anything. Her heart was racing, and she did not know what to say. He continued:

- You look very beautiful... I have been thinking about us a lot that night...

Rosana could not let him go on.

- Walmir, I do not think we should talk now. It is better that I leave.

- I am sorry, I do not know what I am doing.

She could read in Walmir's eyes the same emotion she was feeling. One more minute together and they would surely be thrown into each other's arms. But Walmir regained control of the situation, as always, better than her.

- I did not want to disturb you... you would better go...

- Until any time - Rosana moved away quickly to hide her tear-filled eyes.

Walmir did not move. He stood there waiting for her to leave the building.

The weeks went by, and Rosana tried to live as best she could. She started going to her parents' house more often, worked out with Gilberto every day, helped Fernanda and João Paulo with their business. Sometimes the three of them would meet at her house to discuss some decision they had to make, but she never went back to the office.

One afternoon, she was lying in the living room listening to music and ended up falling asleep.

Walmir was at work signing some contracts to give to his secretary when he suddenly stopped. He leaned back in his chair and closed his eyes, thinking of Rosana. Her presence was so strong that he could smell her perfume. He imagined she was there, felt the touch of her hand in his hair... felt the warmth of her body...

Rosana opened her eyes and was startled to look around:

-My God! What happened? I was with Walmir... I am sure. I feel his presence... he was in the office, and I was with him... it could not have been a dream; it was so real!

Walmir was unsettled by the feeling he had. Her presence had been very strong. It was hard to get back to work. They could not imagine the extent of the love that united them. After that afternoon, many other strange situations happened to her. Sometimes she would be distracted, involved in something, and suddenly Walmir would invade her mind like a tornado. It was as if he was calling her in some way.

Walmir had the same experiences.

Rosana decided to look for Ms. Helena.

- I don't know how to explain it, but we often seem to meet. I have incredibly real dreams. And on other occasions he comes into my thoughts out of the blue. He even seems to be calling me. I am impressed. With her usual affectionate manner, Ms. Helena replied:

- Rosana, do not be alarmed. It happens. Pay attention: every time our senses are dulled, our spirit regains its freedom. It transports itself wherever it wants or wherever it needs to be.

- Does this mean that when I sleep, I can wish to go anywhere?

- Not exactly. The spirit follows its desires and needs, which are not always the same as those of man. If the reason and usefulness of your desire is the same as the spirit's, then yes, you can be wherever you want to be. But just wishing is not enough.

- So, you mean that many times when I thought I was dreaming, when everything seemed real, it was because it was really happening?

- It could be an encounter.

- I often don't remember any of the conversations I had during these encounters.

Don't get hung up on that kind of memory. When you wake up feeling like you have been with someone, just feel what that encounter has done to you. Listen to your heart. What we often think is intuition is nothing more than something we learn or hear in our sleep. They spent the afternoon together. They talked about love, forgiveness, the soul and moral values, among other things, and Rosana was enthusiastic about the new world she was discovering. She left Helena's house still with many doubts, but with a renewed spirit and a calmer heart. That same night, Rosana went to bed concentrating all her thoughts on Walmir, longing to be with him, and her last memory before falling asleep was the kiss they exchanged. She woke up the next day totally frustrated. There was no indication that she had been with him. No memory or sensation. She laughed at herself and her ignorance and stubbornness.

Rosana gradually managed to overcome her pain and anguish, but there was not a single day that she did not think about Walmir. Sometimes she heard from him through

Fernanda. Many times, she wanted to look for him but, as much as she wanted to, she knew it would be a mistake to try to see him and ended up giving up the idea. And she went on fighting one battle a day. She then realized that she still did not know how strong and determined she was.

One day Gilberto called her early in the morning:

- I want to give you a different invitation. How about we take advantage of the beautiful day to go for a walk in Ibirapuera? It is very quiet there today. Rosana loved the idea, and Gilberto picked her up at home shortly afterwards. It was incredible how deep their friendship had become. He was completely different from the image Rosana had of him when they first met. His company made her feel lighter and more relaxed. They had walked a long way; Rosana asked them to stop because she was thirsty and wanted a coconut water. They were on their way to the snack bar and Gilberto's cell phone rang. Rosana told him to make himself at home and she would buy the coconuts herself.

She was still at the counter waiting for her change when a bad omen struck. Everything that happened next seemed like a scene from a slow-motion movie. She turned and looked at Gilberto. He was still talking on his cell phone when he put one hand to his head in despair. Rosana put aside her money and coconuts and walked over to him. When she approached him, she found him perplexed, without action and with his face contorted by pain. She was so nervous that she just looked at him, frowning questioningly.

He looked at her and uncontrollable tears streamed down his face. He spoke slowly, almost without strength:

- Fernanda was in a car accident. She was taken to hospital. They have not given me any details, but it looks serious.

Rosana thought she was going to faint. The two of them hugged tightly and cried together. Neither of them was in any condition to drive. They took a cab to the hospital.

Chapter 12

When they arrived at the hospital, they found an atmosphere of total consternation. Fernanda had been taken to the operating room and there was still no precise information from the doctors about her condition.

Her parents were inconsolable, and gradually friends arrived, Rosana's parents and Gilberto's parents.

No one could believe what had happened and they were still stunned. The wait for the medical report was agonizing and Rosana called Gilberto to go to the cafeteria to get Fernanda's mother some water.

- Rosana, I can't think straight - said Gilberto with great discouragement.

- I want to believe that everything is going to be all right... but I am scared!

- Let's not jump to conclusions. Fernanda is young, strong and has an immense will to live; she will recover.

- All I can think about is praying...

- That is what we should do!

Time dragged on, and everyone remained silent, anxiously lost in their thoughts.

Many hours later, the surgeon finally entered the waiting room. Fernanda's mother wanted to go to him, but her friends stopped her. Fernanda's father called Gilberto and together they went to find out the news.

Her general condition was very serious. She was in a coma and after surgery she was transferred to the intensive care unit. The doctors had done everything they could and now all that remained was to wait and see how she would react.

It was not until nightfall that Fernanda's friends left. Her parents did not want to leave, but Rosana and Gilberto managed to convince them to go home and rest, with the promise that they would not leave and that they would call if there were any changes in Fernanda's condition.

Gilberto was given permission to enter the ICU quickly and Rosana was left alone. She was exhausted and could not find the strength to do anything. She thought about how meaningless life sometimes seems.

-How many things we stop doing because of fears that have been built up in us for centuries; conventions, rules, standards of conduct... We are born and grow up being programmed to live according to the rules established at some point in time by no one knows who. We often run away from happiness for fear of our attitude or choice being misinterpreted and not meeting the expectations of our social environment, whatever it may be. We carry the weight of guilt in anticipation of action. And all our efforts, all our renunciations, in the face of death lose their meaning. How many dreams has Fernanda stopped living? Will she still have the chance to pursue them?

Rosana felt a presence approaching and looked up. Walmir was coming towards her. She started to cry, stood up and he embraced her tightly. Rosana did not try to control herself; she let all her pain bleed out until her heart felt numb.

No words could express the pain they were feeling. Walmir stayed by Rosana's side until Gilberto returned.

- How is she? - Walmir asked his friend as soon as he appeared.

- I don't know, but I am really scared. She's in a coma and looked so weak... I am shocked by what I saw. My Nanda in that state... - her eyes filled with tears.

- I'll stay with you - said Walmir resolutely.

Gilberto and Rosana just looked at him with immense gratitude. The evening passed slowly, and it was very late when Walmir brought coffee for everyone. He sat down next to Rosana. Gilberto went out for a walk.

- I am worried about you. Do you not want to rest for a while?

- No, Walmir, thank you. I know Fernanda will wake up and I want to be here when she does.

- This is crazy; I still cannot believe it is happening.

Rosana looked at him lovingly:

- So many unbelievable things have happened recently... I feel like I am in another world. We think we always have everything under control, then life comes along and shows us how wrong we are. It is so hard to deal with... comes a feeling of helplessness.

- You are right. When we least expect it, we come across situations that try to take us off the path we have chosen to follow.

- The truth is that life is not the way we want it to be... that sometimes revolts me.

- Certain things may not happen according to our wishes, but we must do the best we can with what we have. Revolt only makes us stagnant and prevents us from growing. Rosana showed a certain frustration:

- How can you be like that? You settle for everything, you accept everything... seems to me that you do not control your life... you barely experience what is going on. Do you not fight for anything? Walmir lowered his head, understanding what she was getting at. He did not think it was time to raise this issue, and he understood that she was old, confused and suffering a lot. She was pleased to see Gilberto turn around and interrupt the conversation.

At dawn Fernanda's father arrived accompanied by a brother and made sure that Gilberto, Rosana and Walmir went home to rest. Walmir left Gilberto at home and then went to take Rosana. When they arrived, he went upstairs and made her take a shower while he prepared some coffee. Shortly afterwards, she arrived in the kitchen with wet hair and wearing a white robe; Walmir felt an irresistible attraction but controlled himself. She did not want to eat anything, and he only said goodbye after making sure Rosana could lie down and sleep.

The next few days were terrible. Fernanda had been in a coma for almost a week. Rosana could not work, and João Paulo made a superhuman effort to look after the company on his own.

She and Gilberto took turns with Fernanda's parents on duty at the hospital, and Walmir was a constant companion.

One day they were having a snack in the hospital canteen when Rosana surprised Walmir:

- This whole situation has made me think a lot. Why do we not admit what we are feeling, Walmir? How long are we going to deny our love, our attraction? He was disconcerted:

- Do you think this is the best time to talk about it?

- We have to talk... does not what is happening mean anything to you?

- I know what you mean. Seeing Nanda in these conditions really makes us think about the meaning of everything we do. But imagine what would happen if everyone started living as if the world was going to end tomorrow? No one would want to take on any commitments or responsibilities. There would certainly be a lot of suffering...

- Or a lot more happiness...

- You know that what you have said does not reflect your true way of looking at life - Walmir challenged her firmly.

She scowled and he continued:

- You think I am scared, don't you?

- Yes.

- You may even be a little bit right. But I do not want to make anyone suffer, especially my wife.

- I can suffer, you can suffer, but she cannot...- said Rosana ironically. Walmir sighed and held Rosana's hand:

- What we are living through is something very special, Rosana, but we do not live alone in the world. You are not like that. You are not the inconsequential person you are trying to make yourself out to be.

- You are denying us the chance to try... and you are doing it because you know that if we go ahead, there will be no turning back. I am sure you have never been reluctant to get involved with a woman. But between you and me, you know that you are not in control of the situation. And that is what makes you afraid. I feel the same way, but we are in different situations... I am not committed to anyone. Forgive me if I am being selfish. And you want to know the truth? We love each other very much, whether you admit it or not.

Walmir was about to say something when he saw Gilberto appear at the entrance to the canteen. He noticed that the look on his face was one of total despair. He felt his body freeze and held Rosana's hands tightly. Only then did she see Gilberto approaching. He spoke with difficulty:

- It is over... Nanda has gone!

Rosana and Walmir got up and the three of them hugged each other, crying a lot.

It was the hardest time they had ever had in their lives, and they would never be the same again after that.

Ms. Helena was with Rosana several times in hospital, but when she arrived at the wake, Rosana felt especially comforted.

- I cannot come to terms with it, Ms. Helena. This is not fair. Nanda was so young, with so much still to live for.

- My dear, your heart is too hurt to understand right now, but you will soon see that Fernanda is gone because she had already fulfilled her mission among us. Let's just pray that she is well and keep her affection, friendship and joie de vivre in our hearts. Let's stay with Gilberto... he needs us too.

When it was all over, Rosana didn't want to go home alone. She asked Gilberto to go with her. Walmir thought about offering but thought it best not to say anything. Rosana and Gilberto had become even closer after Fernanda's accident.

Their support for each other had been fundamental in enabling them to cope without falling into depression.

When they entered Rosana's apartment, they realized the immense void left by Fernanda.

- I do not know how it is going to be from now on, Rosana. I am completely lost.

- I know how you feel. I also cannot imagine what it will be like without Nanda. She was my only great friend, the person with whom I shared everything in life. Nobody knew and understood me like she did.

- What is the point of making plans, life projects... all in vain! - said Gilberto bitterly.

- I wanted so much to ease your pain a little... but I have as many doubts as you do, and I do not know what to say.

- Your company is already a great strength, Rosana. I do not know how I would have coped without you and Walmir. As he said this, he noticed the look on Rosana's face change.

- I am sorry, Rosana, but there is something I would like to ask you: is there something between you and Walmir? I have always noticed an intense atmosphere between you, but Fernanda was very discreet and never told me about it. Rosana was tired and did not want to hide her feelings any longer.

- There is nothing between us, nothing concrete. We felt a very strong attraction, yes, but that is all it was. She did not want to go into details, at least not now. It was too complicated for him to understand everything that had happened.

- Walmir is a great guy! A person of great character and a big heart.

Rosana felt her heart squeeze. Walmir really was someone very special and she admired him very much. "My

God, what am I going to do with this immense love?" - she thought, feeling like crying.

- Why do you not sleep here tonight, Gilberto? I would not want to be alone...

- Of course, I will. But you are going to try to eat something, okay?

- If you come with me, I can try... They both smiled and went to prepare a snack. They did not actually eat much, but they talked a lot, and the tension eased. Eventually, they gave in to tiredness and went to sleep. When Gilberto entered the room that Fernanda had occupied when she slept at Rosana's house, he felt immense sadness. He fell asleep with tears in his eyes.

Little by little, everyone tried to get back to their routines. But Rosana did not think she would ever be able to get on with her life again. Everything she did seemed meaningless, and she felt like she was going nowhere. Even work no longer engaged her. João Paulo became a tireless warrior, running the business practically on his own. For Rosana, the charm was gone. She had no one to vent her feelings to and felt extremely alone. She decided to call Ms. Helena:

- How are you doing, Rosana?

- Not very well; I feel so lost...

-Why do you not come over and have a chat? Rosana accepted the invitation on the spot and went to meet Ms. Helena at the end of the day.

- What is going on, my child? You are really down.

- Everything has lost its meaning for me. You know about my history with Walmir. I can't have the man I love; I have lost my great friend... I feel as if I have nothing left to live for. My parents have their own lives, I have not had any children, my work has lost its meaning. I am not finding a good reason to fight for anything. It feels like I am totally expendable to the world.

- Do not say that my dear. If you are here, it is because your presence is important and necessary. You still have so much to learn and teach. It seems impossible now, but you will find your way. Just as life takes away precious possessions, it also beckons us with new opportunities, and we must be vigilant not to miss them. Everything that is happening in your life has a purpose. At first, everyone's reaction is to rebel and not understand so much suffering and injustice.

- But then, little by little, the spirit finds the answers, and our soul finds peace and happiness. What you cannot do is shirk your responsibility to learn and improve. Don't turn your back on knowledge, however difficult it may be to acquire. You will become a stronger person at the end of it all and certainly more mature and beautiful.

- I have been so lost, Ms. Helena, that I have been doing things that I have always condemned. The other day I pressured Walmir to cheat on his wife so that we could live out our love... I am ashamed!

- Rosana, love is something that must be lived entirely. You cannot demand someone's presence, let alone their feelings. He does not feel safe to admit how he feels about you, and he has his reasons for doing so. It is up to you to respect them. How would you feel knowing that he could be on your side because he was cornered by you? A relationship between two people is sublime; it cannot exist based on demands. Remember the meeting here at home? What did your grandmother say? you have a lot to learn before you can experience such intense love.

- I think I understand, but for now I cannot see how to do it.

- Just as Walmir has new responsibilities in this life, you will find yours too. Everything is still very new; give it time. But a good start for you to find your way again is to accept that Walmir has chosen the path he wants or thinks he should follow. Remember that in the past you gave up on everything and did not believe in his love. Do not doubt it now! We cannot always do what we really want.

- I just want to stop suffering... It hurts too much to be without him.

- Pray for you. May you both find peace and happiness.

- Nanda once told me that - said Rosana, sighing.

- She was right. When he has to come back to you, it will happen naturally. But you can be sure that your story is not over. But do not dwell on it; just cherish that love and live your life. The longer we take to learn the lessons that life offers us, the more we postpone our happiness. Rosana left feeling a little more relieved, but she still could not understand how she could accept not fighting for Walmir.

Chapter 13

After the one-year anniversary of Fernanda's death, Gilberto seemed to be getting back to his normal rhythm of life. During this period, he suffered a lot and had Walmir's full support and friendship. Rosana was also a constant presence, but because she was as fragile as he was, she often felt unable to do anything to help. She tried to immerse herself in her work but knew that her performance was far below her real capacity. She had never met Walmir in private again. They saw each other often, but in casual encounters. Sometimes they stopped to chat, but they spoke little and touched on superficial subjects. They tried to maintain a friendly relationship, but the way he avoided getting closer to them made Rosana certain that, despite so much time having passed, he was still afraid to get involved. She even thought that she had deluded herself, that he did not really love her, that he was not attracted to her and that was why he avoided her. But no matter how much he disguised it, his feelings for her were clear in his eyes. Often, when she arrived at the office, she would see Walmir and change direction to avoid talking to him; she always noticed that he would follow her gaze on these occasions. And even with the little contact they were having, the sensations she had talked about with Ms. Helena continued. The spiritual connection between them was too strong.

João Paulo was waiting for Rosana to assess the progress of the business. Despite so many problems, the company was doing very well, and João Paulo was managing everything with determination and perseverance. When they sat down to talk, he noticed that Rosana remained apathetic, showing no interest in the subject. There was no point in continuing and he decided to speak frankly:

- You are not paying attention to anything I say... She looked at him despondently:

- I am sorry, I do not know what is happening to me. I don't really feel involved in anything...

- Rosana, it is your company; you cannot abandon it like this! It is a dream you have been able to fulfill; your clients admire your work and miss the fact that you are more involved.

- I know that Fernanda's departure has left you very upset, but you need to react. It has been so long... She thought of Fernanda and missed her terribly. But that was not the only reason she was so down. She knew she needed to take a new direction in life. The wonderful love she felt for Walmir was turning into a negative feeling that made her suffer, lose her mind, and she was beginning to realize that this could destroy her life.

- João Paulo, you are right. This company is too important for me to put it at risk now. But I will be honest with you: I no longer feel the same enthusiasm for the business as I did at the beginning. I see you so committed, doing everything yourself with such gusto... then I realize that I am totally expendable now.

- Do not say that. Clients come to us because you have credibility in the market. Your name is respected, and your track record is one of success, you know that.

That may be. I spent a good part of my life working to achieve the position of respected professional. But everything has changed. I think if I could live again, I would do a lot of things differently.

- But you have always been passionate about your work.

- When I graduated, I had lots of dreams and plans. When you are twenty, you imagine, idealize and plan your whole life. But we often realize later that all those plans no longer have a place in our reality. I had a hard time admitting it, but I must face up to the fact that none of it makes me happy today. I need to change; I want to change. João Paulo was surprised and worried by what he was hearing.

- What exactly do you mean by that? Are you going to close the company?

- No, but I have a proposal for you. Do you want to buy it?

- Rosana, what kind of idea is that?

- Do you think you can get a partner?

- Wow, you have taken me completely by surprise. I do not know, I need to see if I can make this decision. I really will need a partner.

- Think about it and then we'll talk.

- And what do you intend to do?

- I don't know yet...

- I am worried about you, Rosana. I think it is best to leave things as they are until you think things over. In two years, this is the second time you have taken radical action.

- No, João Paulo, it is not necessary. My decision has been made. All you must do is tell me if you want to keep the company.

Think about it carefully. I am going to get rid of it anyway, and I would rather it stayed with someone I trust and who I know can make it grow even more.

- All right Rosana, if you insist on this idea... just give me a few days to sort everything out.

- No problem; it is not that urgent. I will talk to you at the end of the week. I do not think I will be back here for a few days. If anything more important happens, you will find me at home or on my cell phone.

- Don't worry. You and Fernanda have put together a very good team and everything is under control.

- I will wait for your reply then. As she was leaving, Rosana ran into Gilberto. He had just left Walmir's office.

- Hi Rosana, how nice to see you now. I missed you! Rosana laughed:

- But we were at the gym together this morning.

- For me, it seems too long to be without your company - he replied with a wink.

- What do you want?

- Are you calling me self-interested?

- It was necessary that I did not know you.

- Okay... I confess! I really want to go out tonight and have dinner in a new restaurant, but all my attempts to find company have been unsuccessful. Rosana frowned at him:

- That was not very flattering of you. He stared at her in silence, expecting to hear yet another refusal.

- But despite your lousy argument for inviting me... I accept! - she replied with a smile.

- You always win me over, Gilberto. I do not know how you do it.

- One day I will tell you the secret.

She slapped him lightly on the arm and they both laughed. They agreed that he would pick her up at home. They said goodbye and left, so distracted that they did not realize they were being watched from a distance by Walmir.

While she was getting ready for dinner, Rosana thought about her friend. How many changes had taken place since she had met him. He had transformed in such a way that she could not believe it. And how much fun he was! When she was with him, Rosana could really relax and forget for a few moments the pain caused by missing Walmir.

As usual, Gilberto arrived on time for their meeting, and they went to the restaurant. Rosana hurried to tell him the news:

- I am going to sell the company.

- What news is that? What are you thinking of doing?

- I do not know yet. But I do know that I do not want to continue working in this area. I am tired of it all. I do not enjoy it anymore.

- You know this change is not going to be easy. It is starting again from scratch.

- I know, but I am not afraid.

- Rosana, I know that we lived together for a long time in a very superficial way, but everything has changed, and we have become good friends; and in the name of this new friendship, I feel entitled, or rather obliged, to say everything, I think.

- You know you can be honest with me, Gilberto; in fact, since Fernanda left, I have really needed someone to be honest with me and with whom I can really open up.

- What worries me about your decision to sell the company is that not long ago you changed everything in your life. You broke up with Roberto, opened the firm... and now you want to change everything again. It seemed that you were happy with what you had achieved. I know there is something serious going on and I am not going to ask you about it. But think carefully about whether this decision is really yours or whether it is the result of something you cannot control.

Rosana remained silent! She felt the need to start again, but was she really tired of her job? Would she do this if Walmir did not exist in her life?

- One day I might be able to tell you about all the things I have been through. There is a connection between some facts and my attitude. But I believe that every event in our lives has a purpose. I could leave everything as it is, but I do not feel happy like this. There are things we really cannot change... so, we must look for new ways.

- I think I know what you mean; I felt that way for a long time after I lost Fernanda. There was nothing that could bring her back. I had to look for a new horizon or choose to spend the rest of my life suffering. It is not easy to accept what cannot be changed. We always think that we will find a way, that we will find a way out, that some miracle will happen. But there comes a time when we can no longer deny the evidence and that is the moment to turn the rudder and change direction. And the funniest thing is that when we muster up the courage to do this, then the miracle happens - he concluded with a smile.

- That is what I am trying to do now. I discovered that my desire was not possible. I analyzed it in every way, I fought to achieve it, but nothing worked.

- That is one of the things I have discovered recently. You must learn to know the mechanisms of life. Perceive its signs.

- I once accused someone of being too complacent because they did not fight for their goals. But surely that person is wiser than me and had already realized what we are only seeing now.

- It is true. Each of us lives at a different evolutionary stage. Some learn more quickly; others, like us... end up suffering more. Rosana gave a sad smile and agreed.

- I have been talking to Ms. Helena a lot. What I used to see as conformism, I now realize is acceptance and learning. It was hard to discover that there is a limit to our dreams. I always thought that anything I wanted, that depended solely on my efforts, I could achieve. But I did not know anything. I got too busy looking after the practical side and forgot to pay attention to the human being, to life, to God.

- And now what? What are you going to do with everything you have learned?

- I believe I am already putting my knowledge into practice, accepting what cannot be changed and recognizing that we cannot place our happiness in someone else's hands. Happiness is a personal achievement. Now I am determined to go in search of that achievement. I just need to find the right road. Gilberto was amazed by Rosana's words and saw himself before a new woman, more mature and serene. He was sure at that moment that he could put his mind at ease about the attitudes she was taking.

- Searching is half the battle - he replied, holding Rosana's hand.

- If you stayed stagnant, it would be dangerous. But you are trying to find your way, and that is already a great sign of growth.

- I do not think my parents will support me this time. They have noticed that I am different, and I do not know how they will react to this new mess I am making. I have always been considered so centered, responsible... am I going to have a crisis every two or three years? - she said, trying to make fun of the situation.

- Don't worry so much. Who does not go into crisis? And you can count on me if it happens again. But give me a truce of at least two years, okay? - he concluded, laughing.

Dinner was pleasant and fun, and they did not worry about anything else. They were still drinking a glass of wine when Rosana got serious again:

- Have you ever wanted to be with Nanda?

He sighed:

- Many times; I even asked God to let me see her, just once. There are so many people who manage it.

- I have tried too. But Ms. Helena explained to me that often we are not prepared for this encounter, or the person we want to see is not allowed to make this kind of approach for some reason. She also said that when we mentalize a person too much, wanting to be with them, we can make them feel distressed and hinder their development. When I heard that, I did not think about it again.

- Even Rosana, I learned that crying is not good either. Did you know that even among incarnate people, our thoughts are greatly influenced?

- I have heard about that, yes - she replied, thinking of the situations she had already experienced with Walmir.

- If you miss someone who is far away and become bitter thinking about them, you could be sending them a negative energy charge, which could affect them and make them sad too, and what is worse, without them understanding why. On the other hand, when you think happily of someone, wishing them good things, a wave of positive energy surrounds them and a feeling of peace fills both your hearts.

- It is true; there are also cases of people who cultivate anger and hatred within themselves, and this kind of thinking ends up generating a highly negative magnetic field between them and the object of their anger. The evil we wish someone else settles in our minds and hearts, attracting negative charges close to us. That is why I do not like to dwell on grudges. It is best to forget and move on.

-I agree with you. Even hatred is bad not only for our spirit but also for our body. When we harbor negative feelings, we age faster. It is not worth it, is it? They made a toast. Rosana felt lighter than she had in a long time. She could even think of Walmir and not feel that pressure in her heart.

They left the restaurant wanting to prolong that pleasant moment.

- Shall we enjoy the evening a little more? Where would you like to go, Rosana?

- How about going bowling?

- Great idea, let's go. As they got into the car, Rosana asked:

- Have you not had anyone all this time Gilberto?

- It depends on what you consider having someone. Many months after what happened, I did go out with someone, but only a few times. I was not ready to start again.

- And now? How do you feel?

- I have not stopped to think about it yet. I loved Nanda very much and made plans to start a family. Today I cannot think about building a life with someone else.

- Can I say something without offending you?

- Of course... if I am offended, you will see soon enough - he replied with a laugh.

- When we first met, I found you very unpleasant. You gave me the impression that you were always judging everyone and invariably putting yourself in a position of superiority. Now that I know you better, I can see that I was wrong.

- I am not infallible, Rosana, but I always try not to judge people and their actions. Everyone knows the reasons for their attitudes, everyone knows their pain. I have lived through experiences that have generated a lot of internal questioning. One of the things is that for a long time I felt insecure, very afraid of losing something in my life. I cannot explain where this fear came from, but it was the cause of my closed temperament. I think I did not want to expose myself.

- Is that why you were so jealous of Nanda?

- Probably. And I ended up learning in a very painful way how wrong I had been. What is the point of being jealous, wanting to control the person you love, being afraid of losing them, if fate can separate whoever it wants when you least expect it?

- So, you are the type to hand everything over to God?

- No, of course not. I chase and fight for what I want. I do my part as best I can. But I accept what is not in my hands to change.

- It is funny, everything we have talked about today seems so easy in theory.

- Imagine the following situation: you see a beautiful bird in your garden every day. You are enchanted by him and start trying to get close to him. Every day you put something in your window for him to eat. He tries the food and comes back every morning to look for more. One day, after a while of keeping this routine, he decides to venture out and comes in through the window, landing on your dining table. When you see him, you are overjoyed and try to win him over. At first, he shies away, but then he even lets you stroke his head. And when he comes to eat in the morning, he always comes in and lets you touch him. One day you are afraid of losing him; that he will be attacked by a stronger bird or get tired of coming back. So, you pick him up and put him in a cage. You are happy, after all, now you will be able to hear him sing whenever you want, you will be able to admire his beauty all the time, and you will be able to give him lots of affection.

-The first few days in the cage, the bird sings happily, but after a while he stops feeding and gradually stops singing. You are so safe and used to having him by your side that you do not notice what is happening. You look at him... but you no longer really see him. You met his physical needs by providing him with food and water... but you no longer fed his heart. You could not understand that he needed to be free. It is so normal to have him around that you do not pay much attention anymore. The next thing you know, the bird is dead. Do you know his name?

- I do not.

- Love!

Rosana got goosebumps. She looked at Gilberto with admiration. It was very difficult to see a man with such sensitivity.

- What a beautiful story, Gilberto.

- I think so too, and from it I realized that I still have a lot to learn about love. In fact, there is always a lot to learn. I feel very sorry for people who think they know the truth; they turn out to be the most ignorant of all, because they always refuse to learn.

They arrived at the bowling alley and put serious matters aside. They played until they were exhausted. It was almost midnight when they decided to leave.

- You are a bad bowler, Ro - said Gilberto with a laugh.

- Am I that bad? It was a very lucky day for you. I want a rematch, and I am going to make you shut up!

- It is a deal. I will pay to see.

- I am really hungry, Gilberto - she said, grimacing and pressing her stomach.

- You play badly and eat a lot... What a night! She glared at him; he quickly hugged her, joking that he was defending himself. They went to the café that Rosana liked to go to in the early hours of the morning.

It was getting light when he dropped her off at home.

- Gilberto, I loved the evening. I really did.

- I loved it too. We will do it again.

- I am sure we will. I just have a concern that I do not know how to resolve.

- If I can help...

- You know what it is: I have a "personal trainer" who is very angry. And I am not going to show up for tomorrow's class after tonight. He is going to be a beast. Gilberto scratched his chin gravely and replied:

- My intuition tells me that your teacher will appreciate it if he has the day off tomorrow - he said, winking at her.

- Yeah, maybe he will not be so mad!

She kissed Gilberto on the cheek and went home. When she entered the apartment, Rosana turned on the stereo and went to take a shower. She returned to the living room, opened the curtains and admired the sunrise.

She thought of Walmir. He would be waking up soon. She knew he had a habit of waking up very early. She would have liked to have had the chance to see him fall asleep and wake up next to her. She felt a pang of sadness. But she realized that the pain she felt now was different. It was not squeezing her chest. It was a deep sadness, but it was turning into a softer sensation. She began to remember what had happened since the day she had met him. The horror she felt when she saw him for the first time; her tireless search to find out who he was and to be able to meet him again; the foolish and childish things she had done to try to always be close to him. The night of the kiss...

She was very tired and turned everything off.

-Walmir, how I love you! - was her last thought before falling asleep.

When she woke up, it was almost lunchtime. She got up feeling lazy, washed up and went to make herself a coffee. As she was not going to the office, she ate leisurely and had no plans for the rest of the day.

She had been meaning to tidy up a few things at home for a long time and took the opportunity to start going through dozens of papers, photos and other things that filled several boxes.

In the middle of the afternoon the phone rang; it was Ms. Helena.

- Rosana, how are you, my dear?

- I am fine, thank you. And you?

- I am very well. When are you coming home? You disappeared for a while, and we miss you.

- Yes, I will; I also miss the peace that your meetings bring. I will not miss you next week.

- We will be waiting. I dreamt about Fernanda last night. She told me she was happy for you. Has anything new happened? Rosana did not know what Fernanda could have been referring to. Her life was still the same mess as ever.

- No, Ms. Helena; nothing special happened. Strange!

- Well, don't worry about it. If there is anything important she wants to tell you, she will find a way to do it.

- No problem. See you next week then. Cheers. After hanging up, Rosana analyzed Helena's words. She really could not see any new facts that would make Fernanda happy for her.

Chapter 14

-It is a deal! - said João Paulo with a big smile.

Rosana shook his hand, with a sense of accomplishment. She was satisfied and happy.

-I am sure the company is in great hands. The team loves you, João Paulo, and shares our joy.

- Rosana, I will take very good care of everything here. Have you decided what you want to take?

She looked around, and for a few moments a great melancholy took hold of her heart.

- I would like to take some of the decorations... if you do not mind.

- Of course not! Everything here was chosen by you, and it is all yours. I am going to leave you to it, so you can take your time and pick up what you want.

- Thank you, João Paulo. There really are things here that are of great emotional value to me.

- Just don't leave before I get back; I still want to have a cup of coffee with you.

- I will be here. When João Paulo left, Rosana sighed and began to choose what she would take. Each piece she picked up brought back a memory. Practically everything that was there, she had bought together with Walmir during the office renovation. All the moments they had spent together at that time were forever marked.

Rosana felt great sadness and gathered everything up on João Paulo's desk. Just then there was a knock on the living room door. Before she could answer, Walmir came in. She was at a loss for words.

- I ran into João Paulo in the garage, and he told me you were here. Rosana didn't say anything, and the silence was embarrassing. Walmir was disconcerted, but insisted on trying to start a conversation:

- I was surprised when he told me you were leaving. Even Gilberto did not tell me anything.

- Maybe because he did not think it would interest you - she replied with a slight sarcasm, which Walmir noticed but ignored.

- I did not want you to be angry with me. Everything was very difficult for both of us. And it still is...

She looked at him tenderly:

- I am not angry with you. I will not deny that I have had times when I have felt angry - at you, at myself, at life and at God. I felt wronged and hurt. But that has all gone now. Now I understand things I did not understand before, and my heart is more serene. As she spoke, Rosana felt only a great emptiness inside her.

- I am going to miss you here. Where are you going?

- I do not have any plans yet. I was waiting to close the deal with João Paulo so I could start analyzing the possibilities.

- Will we not see each other again? - Walmir asked with sincere bitterness. When she heard this, Rosana realized the reality she was about to face. Her heart started pounding again:

that moment really was goodbye. A lump formed in her throat, and it was difficult to control the tears. She turned her back to Walmir and walked to the window.

- Never is too long, isn't it? We have mutual friends, and I think we will see each other a lot more.

- I am afraid not. Did you know that Gilberto is thinking of leaving São Paulo? He's been offered the chance to open a gym, only it is in Curitiba. Rosana looked at him astonished:

- Are you sure? I met him yesterday and he didn't tell me anything.

- We spoke today and that is when he told me the news. She was disappointed to hear the news from Walmir. She could not understand why Gilberto had not told her anything. But she would think about it later. Walmir looked at the objects she had gathered and approached the table. He picked up the pieces slowly, one by one, looking at them with affection:

- Do you know that I remember every purchase we made?

- Why do you do that? - Rosana asked, feeling weak in the face of his love.

- I am sorry... I was just remembering good times...

At that moment, the feeling that united them came to the surface with all its intensity, and neither of them had the strength to resist:

-Rosana... forgive me... but I want you so much...

- Walmir, my love... I want you more than anything in the world...Their bodies came together in a strong embrace, and they kissed. A kiss that conveyed not only the immense love they felt, but also all the anguish and fear of the future. They walked away without saying a word. They looked at each other with tears that bathed their faces in anticipatory longing... eyes of goodbye!

Rosana picked up her things and left Walmir alone in João Paulo's office. When she got to her car, Rosana could not stand it any longer and cried a lot.

She went straight home, and when she opened the door, she found a note on the floor:

-Ro, I stopped by to ask you out. I have a lot to tell you, and I cannot wait. Call me as soon as you arrive. I will be home. Big kiss, Gilberto.

Rosana did not want to think about Walmir anymore. She took a shower and then called Gilberto.

- Ro, I have been looking for you all day.

- I went to settle everything with João Paulo. Now I am really free to start again.

- If you are happy, I am happy too. I have some news for you. Are we going out today?

Rosana thought it best to omit the fact that Walmir had already told her about the move to Curitiba.

- Too bad, Gilberto, it will not work today. Since last week I have arranged to go to Ms. Helena's house. And there is a meeting today.

- That is great. I have not seen her in a while either. We could go together and then go out, what do you think?

- Perfect. Pick me up at 6pm then?

- Okay. See you soon. Kisses.

When they arrived at Ms. Helena's house, they were greeted with great joy. Before the meeting began, they talked a lot, and Ms. Helena showered them with affection and attention. Rosana asked her about the dream she had had about Fernanda, but she said she had not dreamt about her anymore. Intimately, both Rosana and Gilberto hoped to receive a message and were secretly looking forward to it. The meeting began and Rosana prayed that her life would take a turn for the better and that she would find the peace and tranquility she had lost for so long. There was a spiritual visitation during the meeting, but nothing to do with Fernanda. The disappointment they felt was soon replaced by serenity in their souls, a feeling that was always present after the meeting. When they left, Gilberto and Rosana went to a bar and only when they arrived did they start talking about their lives and plans.

- So, Gilberto, you said you had something new to tell me...

- That is true. I only did not tell you before because I wanted to be sure of my decision. I will be going through quite a change too.

- Wow, I am curious. It sounds really good!

- You bet it does. I am opening my gym in Curitiba.

- Curitiba? I am happy for you, it has always been your dream, but why not here in São Paulo?

- Here the market is saturated, although there is always a place in the sun for everyone. But I like Curitiba, the climate, it is a modern city but still retains a tranquility that we have lost here. And a friend of mine called me from there to say that there was a gym set up for sale at a fantastic price. The owner was moving abroad and was in a hurry to get rid of the business. It was such a good offer that it did not take me long to decide. It is all settled. Shall we have a toast?

- Congratulations Gilberto! At least one of us has made amends.

- Don't worry, I am sure you will be giving me some good news soon.

- Is this friend of yours going to be your partner?

- No, he just brokered the deal. I will not have a partner as long as I can stand on my own two feet. When are you going there?

- I think in about three weeks. But if I could, I would go tomorrow. I am looking forward to taking over everything. At that moment, Rosana felt a twinge of sadness but paid it no mind. Gilberto continued:

- And you, Ro, do you have any idea what you are going to do?

- Not yet. I was just thinking that I am going to lose my best personal trainer... - she said, making a sad face.

Gilberto held Rosana's hand gently:

- I am sorry, I had not thought of that. But you can be sure that you will always have your friend. I often go to São Paulo to see my parents, and Curitiba is very close by. You can come and visit me too. And I have a friend who is an excellent professional and I will give you his phone number so you can talk; maybe you can continue training with him.

- Thank you, but it will certainly be very different. You know what? I am really going to miss you.

- I will miss you too. But you will promise me that we will always be in touch, even if it is by phone or e-mail.

- Of course... I want to know everything.

- And I want to know all about you too and how things are going here.

- Gilberto, you were with Walmir today, weren't you? He nodded and looked at her questioningly:

- Was he with you?

- He stopped by my office when I was picking up some things. He told me you had been there.

- I actually went to say goodbye to him. I do not think I will have much time between now and then, and I thought I would better start telling my friends about my move.

- I feel so much like talking to you... about things that happened to me... everything that only Fernanda knew, and you always suspected...

- Ro, only talk if you really feel like it. You are right, I always knew there was something serious going on in your life, but as I told you once, I thought it best never to ask.

- But now I want to tell you; I am not sure why, but I really want to.

- If it is good for you, I will listen.

Rosana began to relate the facts from the beginning, calmly and in detail. Gilberto listened to her very carefully, and when he had any questions, he asked right away. He was impressed by Rosana and Walmir's story, but he did not think it was any kind of insanity on her part.

- And that is what happened. That is why my life over the last two years has been so tumultuous. At times I thought I was going to go mad with this story.

- Rosana, I am stunned. It is amazing that all this happened right in front of me and I never realized how intense it was. When I asked you if there was anything between you and you said it was just an attraction that came to nothing, I was satisfied and truly believed it was just that. You must be suffering a lot...

- Actually, the worst is over; when I didn't understand what was happening, I thought I was losing my mind.

- What your grandmother said was wonderful and put an end to your anguish.

- More or less. I came to understand that feeling of knowing him when I saw him for the first time, I understood my dreams and my love for him. But I still think: what is the point of knowing all this?

Gilberto remained silent for a few moments and then spoke calmly:

- I think it is for the best. You have understood why everything happened and can assess the situation better. You have understood that with your attitude in the past you ended up postponing your meeting, and now you will have to bear the consequences of your own actions.

- But is it fair to have to pay for something I didn't even remember doing? Today I am Rosana, why should I have to pay for Innocence's mistakes? - she said in a tone of indignation.

- Rosana and Innocence are the same person, or rather, the same spirit. You are not paying for anyone else's mistakes. They are your mistakes. You sound like someone who does not believe in multiple lives... in spiritual existence.

- Do you know what happens? I have learned a lot, but even so, sometimes it is hard to accept.

- I don't know how good it is to know about our past. But I would like to know where my insecurity comes from, my fear of losing what I have achieved in life. As it was at the time of Fernanda. But do you know that I have noticed that this has improved a lot?

- I hope so, but you will only know the day you fall in love again.

- I don't know if that will happen... - Don't say that, Gilberto. You are so young; do you really think you are going to spend the rest of your life alone?

- Will you? They both looked at each other and started laughing. How could one of them question the other about things he could not answer about his own life?

- Yes, what a situation we are in. As my grandmother used to say: "The broken speak of the ragged" - said Rosana, laughing.

- It is true. We are in a very similar situation. And now, how will you and Walmir be after this morning?

- That was the last time we saw each other. I do not have the heart to interfere in a marriage, and I think he will end up living happily with his wife. And from what Ms. Helena said, they really have to live a story together.

- Rosana, it seems he has been omitting some very important details... I don't know if I should tell you...

- What happened? Has he said anything to you?

- No, he has always been very discreet about you. But it is something that I think will hurt you even more...

- Please tell me. I think that after everything I have been through, nothing can hurt me more.

- Well, he did not ask me to keep it a secret, so all I really care about is you.

- Gilberto, please tell me what happened!

He slowly took a sip of his drink, while considering whether he should really tell Rosana what he knew. He decided he could not hide something so important from someone who trusted him so much. He got straight to the point:

-Ro, there is no other way to say it than directly: Cristina is pregnant.

Rosana looked at him petrified. She could not say anything for a few moments. Gilberto worried about her reaction but said nothing either. A few minutes later, still in silence, Gilberto saw the first tears streaming down Rosana's now upset face. He regretted opening his mouth, but it was too late. He took Rosana's two hands between his and spoke lovingly:

- I am sorry Ro; I could not have caused you any more pain.

She managed to speak very quietly and slowly:

- Do not blame yourself; I would have found out sooner or later. It is better this way... now it is clear that we will not have a future together. I have to come to terms with it and forget about it...

She hesitated for a moment, then asked the question whose answer she had been dreading:

- Is he very happy?

Gilberto did not say anything, but the look in his eyes answered everything, and Rosana leaned back in her chair with great discouragement.

- We never know the twists and turns that life takes, Rosana... no one knows what tomorrow will be like? - he said, trying to cheer up her friend a little.

- No Gilberto, we will not have a tomorrow.

- I am the only one who can say that... I will not have Nanda anymore.

- From what we were saying just now, even you can't say that, can you?

- Well, I have to agree with that... who knows, maybe some other time we will all be together again...

Chapter 15

Rosana was walking calmly through the mall when she stopped in front of a store selling paintings and painting supplies. She spent a few moments admiring the canvases in the window and then went in. After almost an hour chatting at length with the sales assistant, she left loaded down with canvases, brushes, paints and a suitcase in which she would carefully organize everything. And an immense joy filled her chest.

While Rosana could not find a direction for her life, she gave herself entirely to painting. Although she had learned a little more about patience, she chose to paint with acrylic paint, which dried quickly, and she did not have to wait long to see the results of her work. Before long, she had several canvases finished, and with a quality that surprised her. She could not have imagined the extent of her talent.

Gilberto was doing very well at the gym and emailed her frequently, often more than once a day. This kept them communicating and they felt close, one always encouraging and supporting the other.

One day Rosana took some of her paintings to a specialty store to sell them on consignment. As she was negotiating with the store owner, a lady approached Rosana:

- Good afternoon. Sorry to interrupt, but are those your paintings? Rosana looked at her intrigued and replied:

- Yes, they are. I am leaving them here to be sold. The woman looked at the canvases again with a very analytical expression; then she turned to Rosana again:

- First of all, I would like to introduce myself. My name is Maria Pia. My husband and I have an art gallery, and I found your work really good. Rosana felt proud and quite surprised. She realized that she could paint better than she had imagined, but she did not think that any gallery owner would be that interested. Maria Pia continued:

- We are organizing a group exhibition, and I would like you to pay us a visit. My husband will like your work.

- Wow, thank you so much! I would be delighted to come.

- I do not suppose you have a catalog of your paintings?

- Not really - replied Rosana.

- If you could take some canvases for him to see... Rosana looked at the store owner, and he realized that the deal with her was off before it had even been concluded. Maria Pia gave him a business card and arranged to meet her the following day. In the evening, Rosana called Gilberto from home:

- Hi Gilberto, you have no idea what happened to me today. The owner of an art gallery saw my paintings and made an appointment with me for tomorrow; can you believe it?

- That is great! Does this mean that you are now going to be famous as a painter?

- Of course not - said Rosana, laughing.

- If I manage to sell a painting, I will be happy enough.

- Don't underestimate yourself; if this lady is interested, you can be sure that you are very good. I am sure she knows a lot more about the subject than the two of us put together.

- Maybe... but I can't believe it. It seems she wants me to take part in an exhibition.

- Rosana, maybe this is the path you were trying to find - said Gilberto with conviction.

- No, it cannot be; I cannot think of making a living from painting.

- Why not? So many people live like that.

- But I am not a professional.

- You could be.

- It is a bit late for me to think about such a radical change, do you not think?

- No, I do not think so. I know people who are older than you who have decided to leave the profession of a lifetime and change business. If you are responsible and aware of the challenge, of course it can work. And if you want, you could do something on the side at first, until you feel more confident about painting. Rosana wondered:

- That may be, but we are getting too far ahead of ourselves; I don't even know exactly what the meeting will be like tomorrow. I will let you know when I get home.

- I will be looking forward to it.

- How are you? How are you at the gym?

- I'm Loving it. I just did not imagine that I would have to think about changes so soon.

- What do you mean? Has something gone wrong? - Rosana asked apprehensively.

- No, Ro, don't worry, everything is fine. It is just that in this business, there are always many new developments, and I have seen new equipment that would be interesting to have here. But I must take it easy. I have heard of a lot of people who have lost their companies because they went too far. I must take care of the finances, otherwise everything will go wrong.

- You are right, you need to plan and be careful not to take a step too far. And a partner, you are not even thinking about that?

If I can avoid it, I would rather stay alone. Partnership is a very complicated and difficult thing.

- I hope everything works out. As well as being an excellent professional, you are also proving to be an excellent administrator.

Gilberto laughed and thanked him for the compliment. Then he asked:

- What are you doing this weekend?

- I don't think anything special, why?

- Shall we go out for dinner? Rosana was very happy:

- How nice Gilberto, when are you arriving?

- Friday, early afternoon. I am going straight to my parents' house. We could go out in the evening, what do you think?

- Perfect! I am glad you are coming. I miss you.

- I miss you too.

The next morning, Rosana took her favorite paintings, put them in the car and went to meet Maria Pia. When she arrived, she was introduced to her husband, Rubens, a very nice, polite and cultured man. After a short time talking, Rosana realized that she was meeting serious people and felt confident about the outcome of the meeting. Rubens was very impressed by Rosana's talent and surprised that it had taken her so many years to discover her potential. But in any case, he knew many cases of people who discovered their talents at a mature age and were very successful. They talked for a long time and Rosana got to know the gallery and the exhibition project in more detail. She was excited by the idea of exhibiting her paintings but still dizzy with the novelty. They closed the contract and agreed that Rosana would enter eight paintings. The event would take place in a week, and she did not know how she was going to control her anxiety.

On Friday, as soon as Gilberto arrived in São Paulo, he called her, and they set a time to meet. While Rosana was getting ready to leave, she looked at some invitations Maria Pia had given her to give to her guests. She wondered if she should take one for Walmir, but thought it would not be good for either of them, and his presence might make her even more nervous. She took only one invitation and put it in her handbag to show Gilberto. She knew he would not be in São Paulo at the time, but she just wanted him to see how beautiful and well-kept the gallery's work was. When they met, there was great joy. Gilberto looked carefully at all the material in the exhibition and was very pleased. They talked a lot and were excited, but at a certain moment Rosana noticed a trace of concern in him.

- What is going on, Gilberto? I noticed that you looked lost in thought just now.

- It is no big deal. It is just that I cannot entirely detach myself from business, I am sorry.

- Is it still the question of equipment that is worrying you?

- Yes, it is. The gym is doing well, the students are happy, and we get new enrolments every day. That is exactly why I am so keen to modernize and even expand the space as soon as possible. But as I said, I must be calm.

- Who is responsible for everything in your absence?

- Rodrigo is my manager, a great person and I trust him completely. Leaving everything in his hands does not worry me.

- Have you thought about taking out a loan?

- Yes, but I am still studying the possibilities - he looked at Rosana with an intense gleam in his eye and concluded with a smile - but you can be sure that I will find a way and leave everything exactly as I want it!

Seeing Gilberto's optimism and strength in achieving his goal, she thought of Walmir. How different they were. She wished Walmir had had the courage to take a risk, to fight, at least to try...

She quickly pushed this thought aside and turned her attention back to Gilberto. When he dropped her off at home, they agreed that he would spend his last night in São Paulo at her house. They wanted to make the most of the time to talk and miss each other.

On Sunday evening Gilberto went to Rosana's house. They made dinner together, exchanged ideas about their plans, and time passed without either of them feeling it. It was late when the phone rang. Gilberto was very close to the handset and spoke to Rosana, who was coming back from the bedroom:

- Do you want me to answer it?

- Please, Gilberto, pick up. I will be right there.

- Ok, he answered, picking up the phone.

- Hello... There was no answer...

- Hello? Who is this? There was silence on the other end of the line. At that moment, Rosana approached him. He gave her a puzzled look:

- Hello? Who do you want to speak to? He looked at Rosana and held out the handset for her to try and find out who it was.

- Please, who is this? - she tried to find out, frowning at Gilberto.

Then she heard breathing, and the person hung up. She stood there not knowing what to think.

- I hate people who do that kind of thing. I could still hear the breathing on the other end.

- I also find it very unpleasant. But let's leave it at that. I am sure they are idlers. Rosana shrugged and they went to put on a DVD. Soon afterwards, they no longer remembered what had happened.

Sitting alone in his living room, Walmir wondered who the man who answered the phone at Rosana's house could be. He was nervous when he called and did not recognize the voice. That really bothered him.

Time passed and before Rosana knew it, it was the day of the exhibition. She was very nervous and thought all the time how nice it would be if Gilberto were there to calm her down. He had called her early in the morning to wish her luck. Her parents and a few friends would be there, but she missed him terribly.

When she arrived at the gallery an hour before the scheduled time on the invitation, she looked carefully at all the works on display and was proud to see her own among so many really beautiful works. As she had always been, Rosana was keeping to a fairly rational view of the situation, and did not allow herself to dream of a night of glory.

The guests arrived and the cocktail began to be served. Many people greeted her, and she had the opportunity to meet many other artists, learn more about techniques and the path of the arts.

She was just talking to the reporter from a magazine specializing in painting when she heard a voice very close to her ear:

- I had no doubt that you would be the star of the evening. Rosana turned around, thinking she was dreaming. When she looked at Gilberto, she had to stop herself from jumping on his neck with joy. He loved her childish way, and laughing, he hugged her tightly, both trying to control their expressions of happiness.

- You adorable madman! When did you arrive?

- About three hours ago. Did you really think I would leave you alone at such a time? Rosana was visibly moved. They did not leave each other's side for a single moment throughout the evening. When the party was over, Maria Pia and Rubens asked Rosana to accompany them to the office. She immediately sought out Gilberto's gaze and asked him to accompany her. When the four of them got together, Rubens was the first to speak:

- Rosana, I know you have no experience in this field, but as we said when we first met, it is a hard road and a lot of work before an artist is recognized. And that should never be a reason for discouragement or giving up, you know?

Rosana looked at Gilberto, already imagining that her career would be very short. Rubens continued:

- On the other hand, there are artists who take a long time to wake up, but when they do, they become a phenomenon and simply explode overnight. And I have to tell you that you belong to that second group - said Rubens, amused by Rosana's astonishment.

- How is that? - she said, feeling her whole body tremble.

- That is exactly what you heard - Gilberto interjected with a big smile.

- From what I understand, you really were the star of the evening - he concluded, seeking the approval of Rubens and Maria Pia.

It was Maria Pia who continued talking while Rosana could not manage a reaction:

- We have seen this happen before, and you can be sure that you are a success. Your eight paintings have been sold!

Rubens turned and picked up a bottle of champagne. They toasted happily and were already making plans for new projects. Rubens and Maria Pia had a wealth of experience and a clinical eye. They knew what they were investing in and were sure they would not regret it.

After a long night of celebrating with Gilberto, his friends and his parents, Rosana arrived home just as dawn was breaking. She would have gone alone, but Gilberto would not allow her to leave him at home. He went with her to her building and when they arrived, he called a cab on his cell phone. While they were waiting, she said:

- I feel like I am living a dream. The night was wonderful; I still cannot believe it.

- You'd better get used to it. Maria Pia and Rubens have lots of plans for you.

- I think I will need some time to take in everything that is happening. Why do you not stay here today?

- I will not be able to stay; in fact, I do not think I will even sleep. I want to see if I can catch one of the first flights to Curitiba.

Rosana was a little disappointed, but she was very grateful to her friend for the effort he had made to be with her at such an important moment in her life.

He said goodbye with the promise that he would keep her informed about the situation at the academy.

She had been really worried and would try to help him in some way.

In a totally unexpected way, Rosana saw her life take a turn she had never thought of. Rubens asked her for new paintings and told her to get ready because, as far as he was concerned, she would have many exhibitions ahead of her. She began to work with such seriousness and determination that she thought of nothing else professionally. She rarely worried about getting a job as an executive. Her routine was always amid paints and brushes; she just could not give up her daily workout. She often felt that this brought her closer to Gilberto, whom she missed very much.

One evening, she was alone listening to music and drinking hot tea when she thought of Walmir. She looked around and remembered the night they had spent together in that same room. Rosana had been so caught up in recent events that only now was she realizing that she no longer thought of him as she used to. She had managed to live her life without him. They had never met again, and she had not even heard from Walmir. This thought made her realize that the love she felt for him still existed and was strong. But something was changing, and she still could not identify what it was. She looked at her phone and thought about calling him, but by that time he would have gone home, and she would only call his office. Deciding not to think about it any longer, she got up and went to her computer to see if there had been any news from Gilberto. When she opened her inbox, she saw an email from him with an attachment. She read the following text:

"Dear Rosana,

I was very reluctant until I decided to send you this email, but then I realized that it is up to you whether you want to keep the attached file. I don't know if I am doing you any harm, you know I would hate myself if I did. But I do know that you do not even remember the photo I am sending you, and I could not get rid of it without your consent. And that is the only reason I am sending it to you; I hope you understand.

I will write more about the news later.

A big kiss with lots of affection

Gilberto".

Rosana reread the message a few times, perhaps unconsciously delaying the moment to see which photo it was; deep down she wondered what she would see. When she decided to open the file, she confirmed her suspicion. It was a photo of her and Walmir, embracing on the night of the opening of her office. As she had not seen him for some time, she felt a strong emotion when she looked at him. As she had not seen him for a long time, her eyes filled with tears, and she could only ask God to help her forget. She took a few minutes to recover and decided to answer Gilberto.

"Dear Gilberto,

Please don't worry about the photo. I really cannot deny the facts or my feelings. But when we meet, I want to tell you about some changes I have noticed in myself. Of course, I got emotional when I opened the file, but you can be sure that you have not done me any harm. I feel that little by little I am managing to let go of everything I experienced after meeting Walmir, and I feel more at ease about it today.

Tomorrow, I want to see if I can pay Ms. Helena a visit. I will let you know if I hear anything. Don't worry about me, I am fine, I really am. Love.

Rosana"

She sent the message and decided to visit some pages on the internet that talked about the great masters of painting. She spent hours reading and admiring the work of great artists such as Delacroix, Chagall, Monet, Kandinsky, Portinari and many others. Every now and then she could not resist opening Walmir's photo again. As she looked at it, she wondered if she should throw it away. She thought she would, but did not have the courage to do so. She looked at Walmir intently... every detail of his face, his body... he was wonderful! She moved her hand closer to the monitor screen, and with her index finger she touched Walmir's image; she ran her fingers all over his face, his hair, as if she were actually caressing him. Her gesture was full of love, affection and tenderness. Although everything turned out completely different from what she had imagined when she first met him, Rosana wanted him to be happy, and she harbored no resentment towards him. She felt sorry for both for the situation they had experienced in the past and the consequences of which they were still suffering today. But she no longer thought about trying to change their fate. She had really come to terms with the fact that she could not be

Walmir's. And now, he was going to be a father, and he would have a happy life with his wife and his son who was about to arrive... it was very likely that he would not even think about her anymore.

She got up and went to wash her face. When she returned, she saved the photo in a folder of her documents, turned off the computer and went to bed.

Chapter 16

Rosana's second exhibition only confirmed the success of the first. This time Gilberto was not with her, but via the internet she kept him informed of all the preparations and results. People started calling to order canvases, invitations came for parties and exhibitions, and soon Rosana was becoming known and familiar with the art world. One evening she received an invitation to have dinner with some friends, also artists, to celebrate the birthday of one of them. It was a simple, relaxed gathering in a restaurant, and Rosana accepted with pleasure. They were all together enjoying themselves when a man stood up from a far table and caught Rosana's eye. It was Walmir, and he was coming towards her. Rosana quickly thought about getting up and going to the bathroom, pretending not to have seen him. But she could not move, let alone look away from him. When he approached, he greeted everyone informally and turned to her:

-Hi Rosana, so nice to meet you. I really wanted to see you to say congratulations. Last week I read a piece about you in the culture section of a newspaper. I was very surprised by your new work. Rosana took a while to reply. One thing she had not got used to yet, and in a way, it irritated her, was Walmir's always polite and polished manner, so controlled that it seemed as if nothing had ever happened between them.

- Thank you - she simply replied.

- Too bad you did not invite me to one of your exhibitions. I would have liked to have seen more of your work. She looked for a tone of irony or something in his words, but he was being sincere. She let her guard down:

- I am sorry; everything happened so quickly that I barely had time to prepare properly. I only called my parents. I did not have time to send out invitations to anyone else among my acquaintances and friends - she said in bewilderment, certain that this excuse was the most ridiculous she had ever heard.

Walmir did not want to talk about it and just congratulated her again on her success, kissed her on the cheek and left.

Rosana felt like disappearing. She had done everything wrong. She had wanted to ask him about his life, about the baby, to stay with him a little longer... but she had behaved like a fool. That reunion left her shaken, and the next day she went to talk to Ms. Helena.

When they met, Ms. Helena realized that Rosana was falling apart again because of the situation with Walmir. She said affectionately:

- Rosana dear, you cannot let yourself get down again now. Your life is going well, you are discovering a new world, and everything is starting to work out. Do not let anything stand in your way now.

- I know you are right, but just when I think Walmir is leaving my life, he reappears, and I cannot remain indifferent to that.

- Have you never told him what you know about your past?

- I mentioned it once, but he did not want to believe me. Fernanda even advised me not to insist. At that moment, Ms. Helena slowly lowered her head, closed her eyes and remained silent for a while. Then she looked at Rosana and said in a very soft voice:

- Do not refuse to open your eyes, my dear. There is no avoiding the fact that after the night, the day will dawn. You can close the windows and curtains, but the sun will be shining outside, regardless of your wishes. It is up to you to decide whether you want to stay in the dark or feel the warmth of life. She stared at Ms. Helena but could not understand exactly what she meant by that. She had not looked for this situation with Walmir; everything had happened unexpectedly. What was she refusing to see? She had already come to terms with not being with Walmir. What else was there to accept?

Rosana spent the rest of the day thinking about her friend's words. She remembered the dream that Ms. Helena had had about Fernanda. Everything was a bit confusing, but Rosana was sure of one thing: she was not going to suffer again because of Walmir. She would not let it happen. She thought about talking to him about everything she had heard from her grandmother, but she knew he would not take any notice or at least would not admit the truth. The best thing to do now was to live her life and let him live his.

Rosana's family has always enjoyed comfort and a good quality of life. Through her work, Rosana managed to build up a good reserve, which gave her peace of mind about her spending. As a good administrator, she always managed to put her money to good use, including the money from the sale of the company. And she was already making some profit from her paintings. But she never thought she would make a living from art alone. She wanted to invest in something that would give her a certain financial return, so that she could devote herself to painting without worry.

One afternoon, she was walking alone through a bookstore when she had the feeling that she had found her life's direction. It was as strong as it was inexplicable, but it did not matter to her. She got into her car and drove to Rubens' gallery. She needed to know about the next plans he had for her. On the way, all she could think about was her new idea, and she felt determined and overjoyed with her project.

She, Rubens and Maria Pia talked a lot, and she had to explain to them that she would need a few days to take care of some private matters. As they did not have any appointments scheduled until the end of the fortnight, there was no problem. She would contact them as soon as she had sorted everything out.

It was almost dark when Rosana got home, packed a handbag with a few changes of clothes, put the essentials in her "*nécessaire*" and set off for the airport. When she got there and saw the flight schedule, she realized that she would not be landing in Curitiba until after 10 p.m. She did not know if Gilberto would be home, so she bought her ticket and thought she would better call him. She wanted to surprise him, and she would find an excuse to find out what he was going to do.

- Hi Gilberto, how are you? I am calling briefly now, but I would like to talk to you later. I have some things to tell you. Are you going straight home from the gym?

- Yes, Rosana, but I do not know what time - he said, analyzing the situation, and then said - you can call me around 10:30 p.m. I will be home.

- Yes, I will; but if I am a bit late, wait for me. I want to talk to you today.

- I am worried... is everything all right?

- Yes, but I want to tell you some news.

- Okay. I will be waiting. Rosana looked for a cafeteria to have a quick snack, stopped by the bookstore and went to the departure lounge.

The flight went smoothly, but Rosana was completely anxious. She had spoken to her parents a few days ago and for the first time they were apprehensive about Rosana's decisions. Now she wondered what they would say about her decision to travel and her plans for the future. She would call them the next morning, as she had left São Paulo without even saying goodbye. The plane landed at Afonso Pena Airport on time and Rosana was one of the first to disembark. She took a cab and gave the driver the address of Gilberto's house, which she did not know yet. When the car pulled up in front of the gate, she got out and stood for a few moments, looking around. The house was beautiful; white with wooden windows painted dark green, and in each window, a flower bed. The garden was large and full of Hydrangeas, and two large Araucaria trees grew in it, imposing and beautiful. The neighborhood was very quiet, residential, and the streets very well kept and clean. Rosana began to think it was paradise and understood why Gilberto was so happy there. She rang the doorbell. Then she heard an internal door opening and footsteps coming towards it. When the latch of the gate moved, her heart beat faster. Gilberto saw her and had no reaction at all:

-Am I too late? - said Rosana with a huge smile. Only then did Gilberto move, taking his friend by the waist and lifting her up as if she were a doll; then he hugged her and went to pick up her handbag, which was lying on the floor next to her. As they entered the house, Gilberto began to speak:

- I could not imagine a more fantastic surprise than this. I was in my room thinking about you and waiting for your call. Wow, I am so glad you are here.

- I must admit that I made this decision very suddenly. When I called you, I was already at the airport. But I wanted to surprise you, like you did me at my exhibition.

- I loved the surprise. But what happened? What made you take this action so suddenly?

- Shall we do something? I can take a shower, and we can talk later...

- Of course! Come with me to your room; of course you are staying here, aren't you?

- If it is an invitation, it is accepted. He slung his arm over Rosana's shoulders, and they walked up the stairs together. He left a soft bath towel on her bed, checked that everything was in order in the suite bathroom and said:

- It is a nice evening for wine. Shall we drink on the balcony?

- That is a great idea.

- Are you hungry?

- No, I had something to eat before I left.

- Good, I will cut up some cheese to go with the wine anyway.

- I will not be long - she ended the conversation with a wink at him.

Gilberto went downstairs and started setting everything up. While he was putting away the drink and the cheese, he wondered what had made Rosana come down there, even more so by surprise. Before long, she appeared, her wet hair falling over her shoulders, wearing a white turtleneck and light blue sweatpants. Her perfume filled the room when she appeared at the foot of the stairs. A soft, pleasant scent. Gilberto was distracted and turned around when he felt her presence.

- You look lovely.

- Thank you, Gilberto. Beautiful and rested - she said with a smile - let me help you with these glasses and plates.

- Let's take them out to the terrace. They put everything on the table and Gilberto went back inside to get napkins and forks for the cheese. When he entered the house, Rosana watched. He looked very handsome too. His hair had grown a little and the gray was more visible. The same silvery effect had already grown on his beard and moustache. He was wearing loose white pants and a black knitted sweater with a V-neck, and he looked very attractive. When she became aware of her thoughts, Rosana shook her head as if to drive them far away.

Gilberto returned, poured Rosana a glass of wine, sat down facing her and, after a toast, asked:

- So, now that we are calm here, what is new?

Rosana laughed:

- You are so curious...

- And was I not supposed to be? - he replied, laughing too.

- You come here late at night, by surprise, say you have suddenly decided to travel, and you do not want me to be curious?

- You will find out soon enough! But first, tell me, how is the situation at the gym?

- I am fine. I have been reworking some plans, and I think I will be able to start a small expansion for now, but I will also be able to buy some new equipment.

- But everything the way you had imagined?

- Not exactly; I do not want to rush into investing more than is safe right now.

- What about the partner idea?

- You always insist on it... but I don't want a partner. Only in case of extreme need.

- What about a female partner? Gilberto was on his back, adjusting the cushion of his chair. He turned defensively:

No, I have already said that I do not want a partner because... - he suddenly stopped talking and looked at her, frowning.

- What did you say?

- I asked if you would accept a female partner instead of a male partner.

- And that partner would be...?

- Me, of course - replied Rosana, smiling and gesturing with her hand to introduce herself.

- Are you kidding?

- Is the idea that bad?

- No, it is not that it is bad. But I do not think you have thought it through. You are going to invest your money in a gym? Were you not thinking of opening something for yourself?

- I do not need to open it; it is already open. And you know I am a great manager. We can make this gym grow so fast that we will soon open a branch, and then maybe a sportswear label, and then...

He laughingly interrupted her:

- And then I will leave everything in your hands and go rest in the Caribbean! With this project of yours, I am going to be a millionaire. She put her hands to her face, admitting that she was going too fast.

-Let's be serious, Gilberto. I have already told you that I am tired of life as an executive. With you, I have regained my taste for sports and today I love everything to do with it. I have the capital to take a good stake, which will help a lot with your plans. I could easily combine this administrative work with my paintings. And you would not have to worry about that anymore, you would just have to do what you like best, which is the lessons and all the technical stuff. Is that not perfect? Gilberto was dumbfounded:

- How long did it take you to plan all this?

- About...5 minutes.

- You are unbelievable! - he concluded, leaning back in his chair, ready to hear the rest of the story.

Rosana told him how she had suddenly had the idea that very afternoon, and how certain she had immediately felt that this was what she wanted to do.

- But it will complicate your life. Running the academy here, with you living in São Paulo.

- I have thought about that too; I can stay in São Paulo and advance several canvases. And periodically, I can come to meet up and do what cannot really be done remotely. With the internet, the rest can be done by email. It is that simple.

- I don't know why I bother. Of course, you have already thought of everything -he said, getting up to get some water and gently patting Rosana on the head. When he returned, he spoke again:

- Is all this really serious?

- Of course it is!

Gilberto sat down, scratched his beard thoughtfully and took a sip of wine. Rosana was quiet, just waiting for his final opinion. A small hint of anxiety began to take hold of her. He gave her a deep look and said calmly:

- The idea is excellent... we can put everything down on paper and confirm the viability of your projection. What do you think? - and smiled.

- I have a few days to stay here. We will do the work calmly so that there are no mistakes. For today, how about we take advantage of the evening by catching up on some lighter topics?

- Perfect. Tomorrow I will go to the gym in the morning, and I will be back soon so we can get started. But we would better not go to bed too late.

- Let's talk some more and then go to bed.

When she woke up the next morning, she immediately noticed that the house was completely silent. All she could hear was the singing of birds playing happily in the garden. She got up slowly, went to the bathroom to do her morning hygiene, put on a robe and went downstairs. She really was alone. She looked at the clock in the pantry and saw that it was almost 9 o'clock. Gilberto must have left very early. She saw a plate on the table covered with a lid; when she lifted it, she saw a generous slice of papaya covered with oats and honey. Next to the plate she found a note:

"*Ro,*

I left early because the first classes start around 6 o'clock. I left some fruit and white cheese for you; I hope I got it right. There is pear juice in the fridge that I made this morning. I should not be long, but if you need anything, just call my cell. It goes without saying, but in any case, make yourself at home. Love,

Gilberto"

She loved the care with which he left everything ready for when she woke up. He took the juice from the fridge, a slice of cheese and went for a walk around the house. Everything was very tidy; surely, he had someone to clean and take care of his clothes. The furniture was rustic, which gave the room a cozy feel. She noticed that he was careful when it came to decorating, but he adorned each space with the minimum necessary and very good taste. On a table next to the sofa, there was a picture frame with his parents' photo, a lamp and a vase with a small plant. In front of the sofa, there was a fireplace which, we could see, had been used not so long ago. On the side wall, a heavy wooden bookcase housed the stereo, many CDs and books. The curtains were light, letting in just a few rays of sunlight, which made the house feel softly bright. The shutters were open, and Rosana could feel the freshness of the morning in every room. Everywhere there was a potted natural plant; in the air there was a subtle, delicious scent that Rosana could not identify where it came from. She returned to the kitchen and reopened the fridge. Lots of vegetables, fruit, isotonic drinks, some cheese and cold cuts showed that Gilberto was trying to maintain a balanced diet.

She looked around and saw a very old telephone set on the worktop in the pantry. She thought about calling him, but thought she would better go upstairs, take a shower and wait for him to come back.

Shortly after 10 a.m., Gilberto arrived. They sat down together in his office and began to draw up plans for the new company. They did a cost survey, an administrative analysis, looked at catalogs of new equipment and when they had finished everything, it was already lunchtime. They decided to go out and went to a famous restaurant in a neighborhood traditionally known for its gastronomy. After lunch they took a stroll around the city, and Rosana was enchanted by everything she saw. It really was a beautiful place, and Gilberto had made an excellent choice in moving, even though Rosana was absolutely in love with her city.

Rosana stayed in Curitiba for a week. She started going to the gym with Gilberto every day, where she took advantage of the opportunity to work out. She was happy to have Gilberto guiding her in her training again. Finally, the day came to return to São Paulo.

- I think it is going to be all right, Gilberto. I am bringing all the documents I need to start my work - said Rosana proudly.

- That is great! But you did not have to worry about transferring the money to my account.

- You know me; I like to sort things out straight away. That way you can get the shopping done quickly. And as soon as I check how things are going over there, I will let you know when I can come back. I have loved every minute of this trip, and I am very happy that you have agreed to my plans.

- I am happy too, Rosana; I am starting to dream about my trip to the Caribbean- he concluded, laughing.

Rosana began to collect her luggage so that Gilberto could take her to the airport. When they arrived, it was getting close to boarding time. She began to feel a restlessness that she could not explain. Gilberto felt strange too, but if they both noticed the other's manner, they did not say anything. They said goodbye with a long hug. When the plane took off, Rosana thought of Walmir. She leaned her head back on the seat, closed her eyes and felt that they were moist. The longing still ran deep.

Chapter 17

Despite the fine drizzle, the landing in São Paulo was smooth and on time. As Rosana was disembarking, an airline employee approached her and said:

- Please, Mrs. Rosana?

- Yes, it's me - replied Rosana, puzzled.

- They asked me to give you these flowers as soon as the plane landed - she said kindly.

Rosana reached out and took the huge bouquet of field flowers, thanked her and the girl walked away. Controlling her curiosity, Rosana waited until she reached the arrivals hall, put her bag on a trolley and picked up the envelope attached to the paper surrounding the beautiful arrangement. It was a card drawn up by the flower shop itself for remote flower deliveries. The text was dictated at the time of ordering and printed on the card:

"*Rosana,*

I have loved the days you have spent here, and I think our academy is just the beginning of great flights! I hope you had a great trip. Love,

Gilberto"

She hugged the flowers happily and went home. When she arrived, she immediately called Gilberto to say how much she had enjoyed the memory. They talked for a long time before saying goodbye.

Rosana divided her time between her paintings and gym matters. She and Gilberto spoke to each other every day, everything was going according to plan. Her social life had calmed down a lot, and she spent a lot of time at home and with her parents, who were now starting to believe again that Rosana had her head on straight.

As she always liked to do when she wanted to relax, Rosana took the car and drove aimlessly around the city, listening to music and enjoying the scenery. She always said that this was her greatest therapy. On one of these outings, she went to the gas station where her life had begun to change completely. She stopped across the street and just stared for a few moments. She could hardly believe everything that had happened. This time, she had not expected to meet Walmir. In fact, she did not want to see him at all. She started the car and continued her drive. As she drove, she thought about Gilberto, and how good everything that was happening to her was. And the image of him, on the first night she spent in Curitiba, came back to her mind. She drove to the park where they used to run together, got out of the car, sat down on the grass and stared at the large lake in front of her. She began to feel uncomfortable with certain thoughts she had about Gilberto. She realized that she was now looking at him with the eyes of a woman, not just as a friend. When she was at his house, she felt a new attraction, a desire to be closer to him, but she did not accept this idea and tried not to give vent to her feelings.

She started walking through the park and thought about Walmir. She had no doubt about her feelings for him, but the memory of Gilberto now left her confused. It was no use: the more she thought, the less she found the answer she wanted. She returned home, letting her thoughts fly freely through her head. Consistent or not.

As time went by, Rosana tried not to analyze anything anymore, she just wanted to feel free and calm to live. Sometimes she was overcome by a certain melancholy, but she had learned to live with it and did not let sadness dominate her. It was very difficult for there to be a single day when she did not think of Walmir, but little by little these memories began to fade.

The day to return to Curitiba was approaching, and Rosana was excited about the trip. She did not want to create any contractual ties with Maria Pia and Rubens, precisely so that she would have the autonomy to act according to her needs. She was very excited about meeting Gilberto again, but she could not help thinking about her new feelings towards him, and that worried her.

Before she left, she decided to pay a visit to Ms. Helena:

- Dear Rosana, how happy I am to see you looking so well. Your countenance is serene, and the sparkle has returned to your eyes.

- I feel really well. I am just a bit worried about a few things, but nothing you need to worry about. Helena poured Rosana a cup of tea, looked at her and said:

- You have had enough to worry about recently. Now, just live and fight for your happiness. When we hurt someone, we are right to feel remorse. But often we experience guilt without there actually being a real reason for it. We must learn to distinguish between the two situations.

Rosana could not believe what she was saying. How could that be? Ms. Helena guessed exactly what was wrong with

Rosana, who had not said anything about the discomfort she felt when thinking about Gilberto and remembering Fernanda.

Helena did not say anything more about it and Rosana did not want to ask either. Every time they met, Rosana left with the feeling that her friend knew exactly everything that was going on in her life; she even knew what she herself had not yet discovered. And her words always calmed her down and put her on the right track.

As they were saying goodbye, the lady said:

- We make many small changes in our lives, often driven by an inconsequential impulse. And we do this without fear of making a mistake. But when it comes to the big turning point, the definitive one, we always look for many obstacles to mask the inevitable confrontation with our innermost and truest desires. Be happy, my dear. Rosana left feeling light-hearted but not knowing exactly what she would do with the information she had received.

She decided to sleep at his parents' house for a few days, as she was going to be away from São Paulo for longer. She had new plans and needed to decide everything with Gilberto. Her luggage was a little bigger this time; it included, as well as several outfits for various occasions, two canvases and her suitcase of painting materials. She would take the opportunity in Curitiba to paint some local landscapes. When she was at the airport, he met Roberto and had the feeling that he had never had any kind of intimate relationship with him. He was impeccably dressed in a navy-blue suit, and next to him he saw a very tall, blonde woman who looked rather affected, far from elegant. When the woman saw Roberto addressing Rosana, she said something in his ear and went to look in the window of a jewelry store.

- Rosana, you have changed!

She certainly realized that his words were not complimentary. She was very well dressed, but in a totally sporty way, very different from when they were dating.

- You have not changed at all - she replied, anticipating that the conversation would not go any further.

- I have heard a few things about you... - said Roberto, pausing strategically so that she could ask where and how he had heard from her. As he did not notice any interest on Rosana's part, he continued:

- It seems you have decided to go back to your teenage years... every hour inventing something new! A gym? It does not make any sense, Rosana. She could taste the bitterness in Roberto's voice, which was also full of irony and sarcasm. She gave him a disdainful look and said bluntly:

- If you ask me, I think I have really matured now, and I am doing what I really like. I am overjoyed, and I never regret following this new path - she took a deep breath, showing total boredom with the conversation - and to tell you the truth, Roberto, your opinion of me means absolutely nothing. Goodbye, and be happy.

- Page definitely turned - thought Rosana as she walked away.

This time, Gilberto was waiting for her at the airport. As it was still early, they went home, Rosana just left her luggage and went to the gym. The extension work was well underway, and Rosana thought everything was perfect. They spent a few hours in the office studying how the sportswear shop they were going to open would look in a small space next to the cafeteria. There were so many plans that they often had to balance each other's over-enthusiasm. And in this way, everything always worked out.

After work, they decided to go to a supermarket and buy a few things for dinner. Gilberto had set the menu, and Rosana loved this discovery about him: he was a great chef and cooked very well.

When they got home, they went straight into the kitchen, and Gilberto prepared a chicken fillet with herb and mushroom sauce accompanied by a green salad and white wine. Before they started dinner, he went into the living room, lit the fireplace, changed the CD to soft instrumental music and only then did they sit down to eat. For a few moments, Rosana remained silent, savoring not only the food, but also every detail of that incredibly perfect moment.

Winter was approaching and the cold was already intensifying. When they got up, they went into the living room, arranged some cushions on the floor and sat down in front of the fireplace. They had agreed not to talk about business outside office hours, and they kept their promise. Vacillating, Rosana asked:

- How is the heart?

- Still closed. I have not thought about matters of the heart; I am very involved with work and that is fine - he replied, trying to show no interest in the matter.

- But since you brought it up, what about yours? Rosana took a sip of wine and spoke slowly, afraid that her voice would give away her feelings at that moment:

- I am fine too, but like you, I have not given it much thought. She got up and changed the CD again, then changed the subject:

-Tomorrow I am thinking of going to the park to do some painting. Will you need me in the morning?

- No, not at all, you can go without any problems. Here is what we can do: you drop me off at the gym, keep the car, and meet me there afterwards.

- That is perfect for me.

- And after lunch we can think of some nice program to do. I am not going back to the gym on Saturday afternoon. We have until Monday off. Is there anything special you would like to see?

- I would love to take that train trip to Morretes.

- That is a great idea; I have been here so long and still have not been. They say it is a beautiful ride.

- So, do you think it could be tomorrow?

- The Littorina leaves town early; as soon as we wake up, I will call Rodrigo and let him know I will not be there.

- Are you sure it will not interfere with your plans?

- Of course it will...

Rosana looked at him with wide eyes.

- But I am going to love throwing all my plans up in the air and enjoying the walk with you - Gilberto concluded, laughing.

- You are always playing tricks on me... we would better go to sleep then, otherwise we will miss the time in the morning.

- That is true. I will sort out the kitchen.

- Not at all. We will do it together. Let's go and get to work. They washed the dishes, put everything in order and went to bed.

Rosana only switched off the lamp next to her bed when she heard the door to Gilberto's room close. She lay there in the dark for a long time. It was very hard for her to admit, but she was really getting involved with Gilberto. And she could not let that happen under any circumstances, for two undeniable reasons: he had been her best friend's boyfriend, and also because he saw her only as a great friend and companion. And she would not get into another situation to suffer again.

She thought of Ms. Helena and her words at their last meeting. "No, it did not make sense. What she said has nothing to do with this situation between me and Gilberto." Rosana thought, confused.

- There is nothing I can do; he does not see me as a woman, and I need to forget this silly fantasy. She turned over in bed, pulled back the comforter and closed her eyes. She soon fell asleep.

The day dawned beautiful and sunny, but the temperature was very low. Rosana woke up to the distant sound of an alarm clock. She rubbed her eyes and got up. She went to the bathroom, brushed her teeth and realized that the sound was still there. She left her room and leaned against Gilberto's bedroom door. The alarm clock continued its arduous mission of waking him up, to no avail. Rosana smiled and decided to open the door slowly. Perhaps because of the wine from the night before, the intense pace of work and the late hour at which they went to bed, he did not even stir when she came in and switched off the device. She was already leaving the room when she came back and stood at the foot of the bed. She watched him as he slept; he was on his stomach, wearing a dark green tracksuit, his gray hair in disarray on the pillow, his legs and arms slightly apart. She felt like approaching but changed her mind and quietly left. In the kitchen, she prepared a tray with hot, fresh coffee, white cheese, whole meal bread, honey, strawberries and an orange juice. When she returned to the bedroom, he had changed position. He was lying on his side in an almost fetal position. Rosana left the tray on the chest next to the bed and sat down very slowly next to him. She stroked Gilberto's hair lightly, and when she thought about calling out to him, he reached up and took her hand, bringing it to his lips and giving it a gentle kiss.

Rosana's heart almost burst out of her mouth. He said with his eyes still closed:

- That way I will throw away the alarm clock... She was at a loss for words, but she could not lose control:

- Sleepyhead, time to wake up! - she said and got up to get the coffee, placing it next to him.

- We will end up missing the train! When he turned and saw what she had prepared, he could not say a word. He smiled, picked up a strawberry and offered it to her.

Soon they were on their way to the bus station. During the journey, they took several photos and never stopped talking. The impression they had was that they would never run out of things to talk about.

When they arrived in Morretes, they took a look around the town and went to eat, as they were starving. For dessert, Rosana ordered a sweet with chocolate syrup. She was having fun and eating like a child, after all, sweets were not usually on her menu. Suddenly, Gilberto looked at her and started laughing. She did not understand; he put his finger to the corner of her mouth and wiped away a large chocolate stain that had remained there. She laughed and hid her face under the napkin. He gently pulled the cloth from her hands, and for the first time their gazes met deeply. Rosana, completely disconcerted and flustered, ended up dropping her dessert spoon on the floor, which cut short the enchantment of that moment.

They continued for the rest of the walk as if nothing had happened. They did some shopping and returned to Curitiba in the middle of the afternoon. When they got home, it was almost evening, and they both went to take a hot bath to rest their bodies and warm up.

Gilberto was in his room and thinking about what had happened in the restaurant. "I must be going mad; Rosana is a wonderful person, and I cannot risk losing her friendship. I have to control myself, so I do not make a mistake. I could not be feeling this attraction. She is in love with Walmir... I am not going to fantasize and mix things up. I hope she did not get upset with me". Rosana found Gilberto in the corridor. She had a canvas in her hands and her briefcase.

- Do you mind if I go out onto the balcony and paint a bit?

- Of course not. But is it not very cold outside?

- You are right. Can I stay in the living room?

- Come on, I will help you. Is it all right if I lie down on the sofa and read for a while?

- Not at all. Let's go. They went downstairs and set everything up. Rosana put the easel near the fireplace, Gilberto turned on the sound very quietly, picked up his book and lay down on the sofa.

They stood there for hours without exchanging a word. There was a ceremony in the air that had never existed between them before.

Gilberto got up to get some water for both and looked at the painting, which was almost finished. It was one of the landscapes they had seen on their walk that afternoon. He was impressed by Rosana's talent, even though he already knew it. They went to bed, but that night neither of them could fall asleep straight away.

For the rest of Rosana's stay in Curitiba, there was never another moment like the one at the restaurant. The gym store had been opened, the equipment had been installed in the new hall, and they had plenty of reasons to celebrate. Enrolment had risen sharply, and the local media were paying attention to the new meeting point for the city's young people, body and soul. And the day had come for Rosana to return to São Paulo. As she packed her things, she thought about the emptiness that this return represented. For the first time, she had the feeling that she no longer belonged to her city. On one of the many occasions she called her parents, she was informed of their decision to move back to the farm in Bragança Paulista for good. They were tired of the hustle and bustle of São Paulo. But they would keep the apartment for their time there. She packed her suitcase carelessly and, although she was still reluctant to admit it, she really wanted to stay. But she knew it was impossible. There was no point.

She took everything she owned and found Gilberto in the living room. He had just hung the picture she had painted of the landscape on the wall above the fireplace. She smiled with emotion. They were both very quiet and remained so until they arrived at the airport. When they were on their way to check in, Rosana asked him to wait for her for a moment, as she needed to go to the bathroom. She returned and found him turning off his cell phone:

- Ro, I am sorry, but I will not be able to stay until you leave. There was a problem at the gym, and I have to go there now. Rosana was apprehensive:

- Something serious? Do you want me to go with you? - it was all the reason she needed to stay. Disappointed, she heard Gilberto's reply:

- No, not at all. You must not miss your flight. I will sort it out and keep you informed. They left the queue, giving way to the passengers behind them. They hugged and Rosana felt an immense sadness come over her. Gilberto caressed her face and just said:

- Take care. Call me when you arrive.

He turned and headed for the exit gate. Rosana stood and watched, trying to hold back the knot that was forming in her throat. When she realized she could not, she grabbed a handkerchief and returned to the queue, discreetly wiping away the tears that insisted on running down her face. It was her turn to be seen. She handed her ticket and document to the clerk and bent down to fiddle with something in her handbag. She continued to dry her tears; she could not hold them back. She heard the attendant's voice calling her:

- Excuse me, madam, but you will not be able to board. Rosana had the impression that she had not heard correctly:

- I am sorry, but I do not think I understand.

- You cannot board now. Rosana looked at her again, this time in astonishment, and feeling the beginning of a headache, she asked again:

- What is going on? What is wrong? Why can I not board? - she said, recalling in a few seconds the unusual situations that had been reported in the newspapers about people being deceived at airports, and she became tense thinking about what kind of situation she was involved in.

- I cannot give you any details. But here you will have the information you need and who you should contact - and he handed Rosana a piece of paper, accompanied by a very serious facial expression. Rosana moved a little to the side and unfolded the paper:

"You cannot take this plane... Simply because I would not know how to live here or anywhere else in the world without you. I love you with all my might. Don't go... But if you are angry, please do not look back!"

The paper began to shake in Rosana's hands, and now tears were running freely down her cheeks. She slowly turned her head and saw Gilberto standing a few meters away from her with a rose in his hand.

Chapter 18

Rosana and Gilberto were happy together, as neither of them thought possible after so many things they had suffered. There was love between them, a lot of affection, companionship and they discovered that their physical attraction was also intense. Gilberto was a wonderful lover, who always created an atmosphere of romance and tenderness for Rosana, and this made her fall more and more in love.

In a few weeks they decided that they would go to São Paulo together, where Rosana would sort out her affairs, pack her things and leave the city for good. They were also going to talk to her parents about all these changes.

Rosana's parents were delighted with the news and asked about the wedding. They had not yet thought about formalizing the situation they were in, but Gilberto thought it would be important for his mother-in-law and talked to Rosana about setting a date before her parents went to the farm. They agreed to have a very simple ceremony in Curitiba, with only their families present.

While they were arranging everything for Rosana's move, they stayed in her apartment. One day, Gilberto took her to the park on the pretext of going for a walk. When they arrived, Gilberto took her by the hand, and they sat down together on a bench facing the lake. Gilberto began to speak, careful with his words:

- Rosana, in a few days we will be married, and your life will change completely. We have not talked about it, and I do not know if you will be upset, but I think we need to talk...

Rosana looked at him with affection and attention, and he continued:

- We came to São Paulo so that you could resolve whatever was pending here, so that we could start a new life in Curitiba. But there is something inside you that I do not know how it is...

- You are referring to Walmir, aren't you? Gilberto just nodded in silence.

Rosana began to speak, her heart calm, without any fear, and sure of what she was saying:

- You know my story with Walmir. There is nothing new I can add now. I just want you to know that you proved to me that it was possible for me to love someone again and be happy. I cannot deny that Walmir will always be in my life; what happened was too special to pretend it did not exist. Just as I know that in his heart, there will never cease to be a very special place for Fernanda. But I love you, Gilberto; you are my reality, my safe haven, my peace. And what I want most today is to take our business forward and build our life together. And I wish with all my heart that Walmir will also be very happy, as much as I am now with you.

Gilberto looked at her full of admiration and love, pulled her close and kissed her, feeling that nothing would ever be able to keep them apart.

Rosana moved out and they packed up the belongings she did not want to get rid of in Gilberto's house. They did not want to move house and although they took a lot of things with them, the atmosphere remained pleasant, tidy and harmonious. Both their parents arrived, and the wedding took place simply, but it was a beautiful ceremony. Rosana's mother and Gilberto's mother could not hold back their tears, and their hearts were at peace with their children's happiness.

Life went on smoothly for Rosana and Gilberto. The gym was growing and opening branches in other neighborhoods and even in nearby towns. As Rosana had envisioned, they were already starting their own sportswear label. They bought a new building where they set up a garment factory, hired seamstresses and a manager, and the models were created by Gilberto and Rosana personally.

Even with so many things to do, Rosana continued to paint and sell her paintings. Gilberto was a fantastic husband, always anticipating Rosana's wants and needs. He hired someone to help her manage everything more closely, so that she could devote herself more to painting. Time went by and Rosana sometimes stopped to think about how good God was being to her. And she was grateful every day for the life she had.

One afternoon, she was shopping when she felt ill. She called Gilberto and he dropped everything he was doing to pick her up from the supermarket. She did not want to, but he insisted they go straight to the doctor. Rarely did either of them feel ill, and Gilberto was very careful with their health.

After a not very long consultation, the doctor asked them to wait a few minutes. When he returned, he had a serene expression on his face. He sat down in front of them and spoke casually:

- Medicine really is amazing. Not so long ago, it was only possible to find out the sex of a baby after three months of pregnancy. Did you know that nowadays it is possible much earlier? - he concluded with a smile.

Gilberto and Rosana could not believe it. She was pregnant! This was the greatest gift they could receive, and they thought they were going to explode with happiness.

On time and without any problems, Rosana gave birth to Luis Felipe, a beautiful boy like his parents, big and healthy. By then, the family was already living in a new house, just as cozy as the first one, only with more space for the new member, with a swimming pool and lots of toys in the garden.

Rosana and Gilberto were still as much in love as they had been at the beginning of their marriage, and knew that they would grow old happily together, enjoying their son and grandchildren. They just wanted to live peacefully and surrounded by love.

They often received Luis Felipe's paternal and maternal grandparents, who never tired of petting their grandson.

Also coming to visit them whenever she could was Ms. Helena, who became a very dear and welcome presence. One day, she returned from a meeting at a friend's house with a letter for Gilberto and Rosana. It was a psychographic message from Fernanda, in which she said that she was very happy that the two of them were together and that she knew that everything would happen exactly as it did. She asked them to live their lives in peace, because that was their fate. Rosana and Gilberto were very moved and hugged each other with tears in their eyes. And life went on its way... as it should... as it should!

Chapter 19

Rosana was sitting in her garden watching her son play. The morning was cool, the sky was cloudy, and the scent of flowers was everywhere.

As had not happened for a long time, Rosana began to remember the past. Perhaps it was the cold weather; she had always found it funny how the smell of rain and wet earth reminded her of Walmir.

She had never heard from him again, and she just wanted to know if he was all right. She decided to send him a letter. As well as being nostalgic, the manuscript now gave her the feeling of being personal, close and warm.

She asked the nanny to stay with Luis Felipe and went to her room. As she picked up her pen and pad, she hesitated, wondering if she was doing the right thing. But as she began to write, Rosana realized that she did not just want to know the news. Above all, she wanted to open her heart to Walmir as she had never done before; she just wanted him to know...

"Dear Walmir,

I could spend hours searching for the right words to tell you everything I feel, but I have concluded that the best words are those spoken from the heart.

So many years have passed since I saw you for the first time, but when I think back to that moment, I feel as if it happened today. I do not need to close my eyes to see your image walking through that door; an image so clear that I have the impression that if I put my hand out, I could touch it. I remember every detail of every moment I spent with you. I see every feature of your face, your smile, your serious expression of concern every time you realized we were too close.

The strange reaction I had when I saw you, the desire to be with you without even knowing you, the deep pain that afflicted my chest before I even knew anything about you, made me believe that the only coherent explanation for it all was that we had been together in the distant past, and who knows, maybe we will see each other again in the future.

They say that the eyes are the windows to the soul, and I think that is true. Something about you made a deep impression on me: the way you looked at me. While you said you had no feelings for me, that it had all been a mistake, your eyes said exactly the opposite.

You must think that I threw myself into the arms of that feeling in a blind flight. But it was not like that. I fought a lot against myself; I was always looking for details that would show me that I was wrong and that there was no strong connection between us. I looked for evidence of my delusion, my illusion. But when we met and our gazes met, all my struggle went down the drain.

I never mentioned to you that one day, one of those girls from the convenience store, with whom I had never spoken, approached me apologizing for her indiscretion, and asked me if you and I were in love. I wanted to know why she thought that, and do you know what she said? When we were together, everything seemed to sparkle around us, like fireworks. She went on to say that she was not the only one who had noticed it. I thought it was funny, I took it as a joke, but when I left, I was once again sure that the chemistry and energy between us had never been a figment of my imagination.

I still think about it today if we had made love. It would have been an intense, sublime, wonderful moment. We would love each other with our skin and our hearts. My body, my mind and my soul give me this certainty. The emotion and taste of our kiss confirm it.

One day you asked me why you were so important to me. There are many reasons, but I would say that among the main ones is the fact that you made me reborn and become a better person. Through you I discovered faith, courage, determination and humility. I discovered that life is much more and much bigger than what we are used to seeing daily. That every human being is special and deserves respect, even if we do not agree with them sometimes. That judging anyone is a dangerous and unfair act, because everyone knows their history, their pain and their struggles.

I have learned from you to be more responsible and patient. To look at the world with more tolerance. I have understood that I can and must make use of my free will, but also that I must bear the consequences of my choices. God gave us the power to think, to reason, so that we can decide and seek our own happiness. That is what He wants for us. And not to use our intelligence, our perception of the facts and the learning that life gives us, is to remain stagnant; it is a delay in our development.

With you I discovered true love, the kind that asks for nothing.

I learned that jealousy is far from being a demonstration of affection and love; it reflects the insecurity and personal dissatisfaction of those who feel it. A feeling of possession, not love.

True love has nothing to do with platonic love. The latter is never externalized; it lives on fantasies and ideals. The other fights, tries to win their place, believes in the qualities of the one they love, but does not turn a blind eye to their faults. And even when they realize they cannot go on, true love never ceases to exist.

Such is my love for you. Even though I am far away, happy and aware of the path I have chosen, I pray for you every day; I wish you well and happy. I wish you found peace and harmony with your wife and son, just as I did with my family. I thank God for having illuminated my path and placed in it a man as wonderful as Gilberto, a companion for all hours and with whom I know I will live happily until the last of my days.

I still get very emotional about the memories, and if I could I would relive every moment. It is a delicious nostalgia. Of course, it would be a complete fulfillment if I could have lived this love with you. But if that was not possible, I cherish this feeling and everything I learned from you will always be in my heart. You once asked me if you could charge me when I said with conviction that I would forget you. You can ask me, but the answer will be different: I have not managed to forget you. Today I know that our paths are opposite, and I accept that reality with serenity. We have our commitments from the past, you to your family and me to mine, and we must fulfill our missions with love and wisdom.

I owe you a lot! You are a man of great character, a good heart, responsible and honest. You are consistent with your truths. You are sensitive and open to new ideas, always seeking growth and knowledge. All this has won me over even more over time. I have some objects with me that we bought together. They are fragments of a time I do not want to forget. I am at peace and happy to be able to tell you all this. We will continue our journey, but I want you to know that there is someone here who loves you very much and who you can count on whenever you need them. I will never forget that one day you wrote me a note saying that everything works out in the end. Maybe that is the end... You will always be the love of all my lives. And I believe we will meet again in some other life. A big kiss with lots of affection, stay in peace and be very happy.

Rosana."

Zibia Gasparetto's Greatest success stories

With more than 20 million titles sold, the author has contributed to the strengthening of spiritualist literature in the publishing market and to the popularization of spirituality. Learn more of the author's successes.

Romances Dictated by the Spirit Lucius

The Life Force

The Truth of each one

Life knows what it does

She trusted in life

Between Love and War

Esmeralda

Thorns of Time

Eternal Bonds

Nothing is by Chance

Nobody is Nobody's

God's Advocate

Tomorrow Belongs to God

Love Won

Unexpected Encounter

On the Edge of Destiny

The Sly One

The Morro of Illusions

Where is Teresa?

Through the Doors of the Heart

When Life chooses
When the Hour Comes
When it is necessary to return
Opening for Life
Not afraid to live
Only love can do it
We Are All Innocent
Everything has its price
It was all worth it
A real love
Overcoming the past

Other success stories by André Luiz Ruiz and Lucius
The Love Never Forgets You Trilogy
The Strength of Kindness
Under the Hands of Mercy
Saying Goodbye to Earth
At the End of the Last Hour
Sculpting Your Destiny
There are Flowers on the Stones
The Crags are made of Sand

Books of Eliana Machado Coelho and Schellida

Hearts without Destiny

The Shine of Truth

The Right to be Happy

The Return

In the Silence of Passions

Strength to Begin Again

The Certainty of Victory

The Conquest of Peace

Lessons Life Offers

Stronger than Ever

No Rules for Loving

A Diary in Time

A Reason to Live

Eliana Machado Coelho and Schellida, Romances that captivate, teach, move and

can change your life!

Romances of Arandi Gomes Texeira and The Count J.W. Rochester

Lancaster County

The Power of Love

The Trial

Cleopatra's Bracelet

The Reincarnation of a Queen

You Are Gods

Books of Marcelo Cezar and Marco Aurelio

Love is for the Strong

The Last Chance

Nothing is as it Seems

Forever With Me

Only God Knows

You Make Tomorrow

A Breath of Tenderness

Books of Vera Kryzhanovskaia and JW Rochester

The Revenge of the Jew

The Nun of the Marriages

The Sorcerer's Daughter

The Flower of the Swamp

The Divine Wrath

The Legend of the Castle of Montignoso

The Death of the Planet

The Night of Saint Bartholomew

The Revenge of the Jew

Blessed are the poor in spirit

Cobra Capella

Dolores

Trilogy of the Kingdom of Shadows

From Heaven to Earth

Episodes from the Life of Tiberius

Infernal Spell

Herculanum

On the Frontier

Naema, the Witch

In the Castle of Scotland (Trilogy 2)

New Era

The Elixir of Long Life
The Pharaoh Mernephtah
The Lawgivers
The Magicians
The Terrible Phantom
Paradise without Adam
Romance of a Queen
Czech Luminaries
Hidden Narratives
The Nun of the Marriages

Books of Elisa Masselli

There is always a reason
Nothing goes unanswered
Life is made of decisions
The Mission of each one
Something more is needed
The Past does not matter
Destiny in his hands
God was with him
When the past does not pass

Just beginning

Books of Vera Lúcia Marinzeck de Carvalho and Patricia

Violets in the Window
Living in the Spirit World
The Writer's House
Flight of the Seagull

Vera Lúcia Marinzeck de Carvalho and Antônio Carlos

Love your Enemies
Slave Bernardino
the Rock of Lovers
Rosa, the third fatality
Captives and Freed

Books of Mónica de Castro y Leonel

In spite of everything
Love is not to be trifled with
Face to Face with the Truth
Of My Whole Being

I wish

The Price of Being Different

Twins

Giselle, The Inquisitor's Mistress

Greta

Till Life Do You Part

Impulses of the Heart

Jurema of the Jungle

The Actress

The Force of Destiny

Memories that the Wind Brings

Secrets of the Soul

Feeling in One's Own Skin

World Spiritist Institute

www.ingramcontent.com/pod-product-compliance
Lightning Source LLC
LaVergne TN
LVHW041807060526
838201LV00046B/1167